Scientific
Sailboat
Racing

SCIENTIFIC SAILBOAT RACING

by Ted Wells

Thoroughly revised and updated
by Ted Wells and Lowry Lamb

With photographs and drawings

DODD, MEAD & COMPANY

NEW YORK

To Marge

1 2 3 4 5 6 7 8 9 10

Library of Congress Cataloging in Publication Data

Wells, Theodore Arthur, date
    Scientific sailboat racing.

    1. Sailboat Racing.   I. Lamb, Lowry.   II. Title.
GV827.W4 1979   797.1′4   79–13553
ISBN 0–396–07690–4

Introduction

The best thing about racing sailboats as a hobby is that no one is ever so good that he cannot be beaten, and no one is ever so poor that he doesn't have a chance.

The sentence above started the introduction to the first edition of *Scientific Sailboat Racing*. Since this first edition was published in 1950, the construction of boats has undergone a revolution, not only in materials and manufacturing methods, but also in hardware and equipment available. Maintenance is now much less demanding, leaving more time for pleasure—and for learning how to race successfully. The basic principles for racing scientifically have not changed—but there are many new developments and techniques which have evolved. All of these new things will be covered in this third edition of *Scientific Sailboat Racing*. That first paragraph still sums up my opinion on sailboat racing as a hobby, however.

Identical conditions never occur twice—there is always at least a little variation—so there is no chance of getting bored with sailing races. Almost every situation will, however, be followed sometime later—maybe once a month, maybe once a season, or maybe only once every several years—by a new situation just close enough to the previous one so that if you are wide awake, you can profit by what you learned the first time a similar situation occurred. No chance for boredom but a chance to profit by experience.

This book really pertains only to racing of small sailboats. I know nothing about racing big boats—but from what I read about their races in the magazines, it appears that the successful ones are now being sailed with as much attention to detail as small boats are. That should probably not come as a surprise as a lot of the big boat skippers learned their racing in small boats.

When I first started winning races with some consistency some years ago, everyone assumed that it was my experience with airplanes and my supposedly superior knowledge of aerodynamics that was my secret for success. I finally got tired of explaining that a knowledge of theoretical aerodynamics was a hindrance, if anything, and that there wasn't any Arthur-Murray-in-a-Hurry method of learning how to win races, so I wrote the first edition of this book.

I still feel that a technical knowledge of airplanes, or of any other branch of science for that matter, is of no value in learning how to win sailing races, but a scientific and analytical approach to solving the problems of winning races is of the greatest importance. The danger with the scientific approach seems to be that with some people this approach tends to go blindly down one of two alleys—preoccupation with either sails or hull lines, ignoring the people who are in the boat.

Three factors are important in winning races: The boat must be good, the sails must be good, and the skipper-and-crew combination must be good. All are important. It is impossible to say definitely which is the most important—except that there are still too many skippers who don't look in the mirror when they are looking for reasons for not winning races.

A good skipper can trade boats and sails with an inexperienced skipper in a race, and if the boats and sails are not too unequal, the good skipper will beat the inexperienced one in the race by about as big a margin as he would have without trading. Of course, if you are going to take your racing seriously there is no point in handicapping yourself by not having a boat and sails that are as good as the best.

In one-design classes, all boats can be, but frequently aren't, as good as the best. There is no reason, however, why an old boat that is not in completely hopeless condition cannot be made to equal the best, and with a new boat there just should be no reason at all for alibis. Sails, if they have been made by a sailmaker who has a reputation for making good sails for the class you are sailing in, are awfully close to identical. An occasional lemon may show up, but in most cases, the problem is knowing how to use them to the best advantage. Developing a good skipper-and-crew combination is by far the most difficult problem. It requires learning how to get the most out of the boat and sails under all conditions, making the correct tactical decisions almost without thinking, and doing a minimum of dumb things.

It is a good idea to keep notes on your races, listing the sails used, the wind and water conditions, any particularly bright or dumb things done, and what happened and why. Studying these notes frequently will be very valuable—either for the beginner or for the expert. Reviewing this book now and then won't hurt either. It is amazing how things which just slide by the first few times finally ring a bell in the light of later experience.

What scientific sailboat racing really amounts to is to base your conclusions only on facts which have been carefully observed, analyzed, and classified—then to make the most of them.

Contents

III
Racing Tactics

IV
Some Random Reflections from Experience

Illustrations

PART I

Making Your Boat
and Sails Equal
to the Best

1

Tuning the Boat

A POPULAR EXCUSE FOR NOT WINNING RACES IS, "MY BOAT WASN'T TUNED up properly." This implies that there is some deep, dark mystery involved and that if the skipper could only find something on the boat that he could pull, shove, or twist a microscopic amount he would start winning races. This is a lot of baloney. A boat which is in hopelessly bad shape and has never won any races cannot be made good enough to win races with a little twiddling here and there. On the other hand, if a boat has consistently placed well and suddenly starts placing poorly, the chances are pretty good that it isn't the boat that needs tuning up—it is the skipper.

In most one-design classes there is not enough difference between the maximum and minimum permissible dimensions so that there can possibly be any significant difference between boats as a result of differences in hull lines. Many skippers, even those with long experience, will not agree with this statement. As an example, they will point to the fact that a certain skipper who never got near the top bought a new boat and immediately started winning races. Therefore any fool can plainly see that the new boat is a hot one—particularly since it is now beating other boats from the same builder.

The answer to this is, to paraphrase a statement of Charles Kettering's, that the trouble with the skippers jumping to this conclusion is not that they do not know enough, but that they know too many things that are not so. They are probably ignoring the fact that this skipper has good sails, does a good job of sailing, and that anyone else probably would not have finished before dark

3

with the boat he was using before he got the new one.

Another favorite example of these skippers is to point out that a certain boat always does well (or badly) under some particular condition, such as in a very light or very high wind, and the assumption is that this is due to something mysterious about the lines of the boat. The fallacy here is that they are not separating out the important from the unimportant and are taking a supposition for a fact. The fact that the boat consistently wins (or loses) under certain conditions must be accepted as a fact—but the cause may be that the skipper has good sails for only one range of wind velocities, the skipper may be a good light-wind skipper and not know how to handle a boat in high winds (or vice versa), or any one of a number of other things which I hope will become apparent after reading this book.

However, with boats built to identical measurements, there are many things which make the difference between a good racing boat and a clunker, and a tremendous difference in performance can and does exist between boats with identical lines. But none of these things is mysterious and there is no reason why anyone, particularly if he is starting out with a new boat or has an old one which is not in too hopeless a condition, cannot have one which is as good as the best. The best boat is the one on which the owner has done the best job of doing *all* the things that help to make a good boat. Tuning up a boat really involves doing all these things —there isn't any such thing as tuning up a boat to make it a winner by a few minor adjustments. These adjustments are only the finishing touches that are put on after a lot of work.

I am reminded of a violin—properly played and with all strings correctly tensioned, the result is harmony. Therefore, tuning is doing everything necessary to put the boat in proper harmony. I will stress those items that are important in making your boat equal to the best. Many of them will be small, but they are the things that make the difference between an outstanding boat and just a good boat. Very few single things will mean much—it is the cumulative effect of lots of small things that counts.

2

The Most Important Thing of All

BEFORE GOING INTO THE VARIOUS DETAILS OF EQUIPMENT, TACTICS, ETC., let me emphasize that the most important factor in winning races is the skipper. Good crews are necessary but, since it is generally the skipper who makes the decisions, this commentary is directed to him.

You must decide whether you really want to win races. Of course everyone would like to win, but obviously for every first there must be a last. To win requires a tremendous amount of effort. Many a beginning sailor spends a lot of money to get the best equipment, charges out on the race course, and finishes last. The performance is repeated for a few weekends and by the end of the summer he has about given up. He feels he has worked hard, but he really wasn't willing to pay the price.

As with any form of human endeavor, determination is what pays. As a start, assume you know nothing about sailing, then proceed to learn all you can about it. Reading articles and books is the first step. Not that you will understand everything, but at least you will become familiar with the language and ter-minology. Then ask questions. I don't believe I have ever met a good sailor who wasn't willing to talk about sailing and why he has become one of the top men. Many times he will not know (although he thinks he does) and will give you a wrong answer. I recall sailing alongside a middle-of-the-fleet sailor on the first beat. I tacked, left him, and rounded the windward mark in first place; he rounded in last place. After the race the skipper asked me why I had tacked. I could not answer him with other than, "It was time to tack." I did not honestly know. Perhaps it was a wind shift, a tactical position, or maybe one of those "seat-of-the-pants" decisions that comes only with experience.

Do not be afraid to experiment. Change mast position, mast rake, jib sheet location, etc. Knowing measurements of the boats of the better sailors in your class is the perfect place to start. However, the locations for one expert may be just right for his style of sailing but may not be for you. There is also the possibility he may have something wrong and would be a lot faster with a change.

However, all is for naught unless you get lots of practice. The more practice you have, the easier it will be to maintain your self-confidence, and the more confidence you have in your own ability the easier you will find it to win races. Many people on the coasts wonder how skippers sailing on lakes that are not even big enough for a good yacht anchorage can frequently do much better in big regattas than they should. The answer is simple—practice. With short courses and numerous laps, there is lots of practice rounding marks. And where you have to tack every few minutes or run out of lake, you get lots of practice coming about. The boats are bound to be closely grouped—they haven't any place to go—so you get lots of practice on rules and competitive tactics. Also, the skippers are delighted to get a chance to race on somebody else's mud puddle, so they frequently pack their boats on trailers and make round trips of 500 to 1000 miles over a weekend for a regatta. Practice under varying conditions. There is no substitute. An excellent idea for a new skipper is to crew for an experienced skipper any time he gets an opportunity. He can learn a lot this way. Another good idea is to crew for some novice sailors. When they make an error it is quite obvious and can serve to remind you of something that you might be doing. In a light air race one young sailor had overtrimmed his mainsail so much that the mast was bending way out of shape. It took a while to locate the cause of the "slow," but when corrected it made a vast difference. That experience shows that with all the modern free-running blocks, it is easy to overtrim. Doing some time on the race-committee boat or picket boat offers a fine vantage point to observe errors.

Race as often as possible in the stiffest competition you can get. When not racing you can practice starts, tacking, jibing, rounding marks, putting the whisker pole out and taking it in until you and your crew work perfectly as a team.

Keep notes on your experiences in each race for future reviewing. Write down the wind-and-water conditions, sails used, and details on any particularly bright or dumb things that you or anyone else did. You will find that reviewing these notes will be very valuable to refresh your memory, particularly at the start of the season. It will not hurt you any to review this book frequently, too; you will be surprised how some recent experience will give new emphasis to something said here which you did not take in at the time.

3

Hull Construction

IN THE YEARS SINCE THIS BOOK WAS FIRST PUBLISHED, THERE HAS BEEN A vast increase in the number of racing sailboats. This demand was brought about by the development of fiberglass reinforced plastics for hulls, aluminum for spars, and dacron for sails. Boats can now be mass produced, more or less. It would be impossible to have as many boats as we now have if they had to be constructed of wood. There are just not that many skilled craftsmen available, and it takes years to acquire the knowledge needed. The new materials have also taken much of the drudgery out of upkeep. No longer is it necessary to spend weeks sanding and spraying the bottoms, varnishing the decks and spars, and spending many hours gently breaking in a new suit of sails. Perhaps we have been oversold on the time to be saved from work but, in any case, the new era has arrived.

The older classes have seen the transition from wood to fiberglass with mixed emotions. The first fiberglass boats were quite heavy, especially in the ends, and did not prove as competitive as the good wooden boats. The initial attempts to make fiberglass as stiff as wood required many layers of cloth and resin, resulting in too much weight. The use of sandwich construction with core materials such as foam or balsawood has cut the weight, however, and the weight-to-strength ratio is now as good as that for even the lightest wooden boats.

One of the main problems with the use of fiberglass is that, unlike wood, it does not float. From the start it was necessary to design some method to insure that boats did not sink when they capsized. Some classes merely built in air tanks. This was all right if the boat was immediately righted. However, air tanks are not reliable and in some instances boats sank. Now most boats have at least enough foam to float the boat. Foam was first located under the decks and, when full of water, the boat floated much like a wooden one. In either situation, if the boat was capsized and filled with water you were out of the race. A swamped boat such as this can only be bailed in smooth water at a dock or on shore, and it is difficult to tow.

Somewhere along the line, somebody got the idea that by locating the foam in the bottom, you could stiffen the hull and reduce the weight. Then it was just a step further to construct a self-bailing boat. This was a fine idea, since an increasing number of boats on the race course presented the problem of providing enough rescue boats. This was brought to the attention of the International Yacht Racing Union(I.Y.R.U.), and they used their influence to encourage the adoption of methods to enable a boat that was capsized and swamped to be righted and sailed away. Unfortunately, the term "self-rescue" came to be applied to boats built with these abilities. "Self-rescue" connotes that a boat will automatically right itself and remove any water without any effort by the skipper and crew. A better term would be "sail-away capability" which means that a boat can be sailed away as opposed to having to be towed away. No doubt the erroneous term was picked out by some overzealous advertising executive who knew nothing about sailing. The damage has been done, but you should keep in mind that the term is more generic than descriptive.

Apparently some of the classes, as well as the I.Y.R.U., went too far in the amount of flotation required. With too much flotation two problems arose. First, the boat floated quite high in the water and, if the crew did not hang onto it, would be blown away. This could occur if a crew left to retrieve floating gear, instead of staying with the boat until it was righted.

The other problem was the tendency for the boat to turn completely upside down or "turtle," especially when the wind kept blowing on the bottom. An aluminum mast may compound the difficulties, because it soon fills with water. Some masts are supposed to be watertight, but most will not keep water out very long or float very well even if they do not fill with water.

The ideal amount of flotation involves compromises and there is certainly no perfect answer. The I.Y.R.U. put out some recommendations for maximum height after swamping but these were only guides and not mandatory.

A wood boat with no extra flotation or a fiberglass boat with flotation under the deck has the least tendency to turn turtle, is the easiest to right after capsizing, but can be towed and bailed only with extreme difficulty. A boat with its extra flotation primarily in the bottom provides the best self-bailing going to windward because the water accumulates in a well around the bailer and only a quart or so of water provides a pressure head of several inches. This type of hull usually has transom drains also, which facilitates getting rid of larger quantities of water. The disadvantages are that it is harder to right after capsizing because the center of buoyancy when floating on its side is much closer to where the crew is standing on the centerboard; and, because it generally has more than the minimum amount of flotation, it floats higher out of the water when on its side, giving more resistance to the wind, and therefore has more tendency to turn turtle. After righting, the water can be bailed out without too much difficulty.

Another way of providing extra flotation is by built-in side tanks or air bags. This method does not provide the improved self-bailing going to windward unless the boat also has a double bottom, and if it turns turtle it has all the stability of an upside-down catamaran. When on its side it will float high, but the center of buoyancy is farther from the centerboard so it is easier to right. After righting, it will be difficult to sail dry but easy to tow.

So—you pays your money and takes your choice.

The weight of the boat should be as close as possible to the minimum weight permitted. Every effort should be made to keep the weight to the minimum as there is no point in trying to win races without doing everything possible to make it easier to win them.

The effect of excess weight is most noticeable in steady light winds and in a high wind which is just strong enough for a light boat to plane, but not quite strong enough to get a heavier boat up out of the water. Otherwise, in a high wind the detrimental effect of excess weight is less noticeable. In a light shifty wind, being where the wind is is much more important than the weight of the boat, and I have won lots of races in light shifty winds with a boat over the minimum and with crews who were heavy but skillful, by being in the right place at the right time. Some people think that excess weight is an advantage in high winds on the theory that the heavier boat will drive through waves better. The fallacy in this theory is that while the heavy boat will be slowed down less by a wave, it will also accelerate less rapidly after having been slowed down.

The best proof of this that I have ever seen occurred in one of the Snipe Class World Championship races held at Larchmont

Yacht Club in 1949. Each skipper had a different boat each day. The boats could be put in three groups—two which were light and had good bottoms, centerboards, etc.; three which were either heavy but with good underwater characteristics, or reasonably light but lacking good underwater parts; and four about which nothing good could be said.

In one race I had one of the last group, but there was a good breeze and I had a good start and was doing all right on the first windward leg until the wind died, leaving a lumpy sea and practically no means of propulsion. The English boat, which was one of the first group and which I had been staying ahead of successfully, went past me like a six meter while all I did was bounce around. The waves slowed him down, but he kept moving. When I got slowed down, I couldn't get started again. Momentum is mass multiplied by velocity. Mass doesn't do you any good unless you can get velocity.

In another race, I had a boat from the second group. It had a good bottom and a well-sharpened centerboard and rudder but was about 40 pounds overweight. The Argentine boys had one of the first group of boats, and the combined weight of the two boys was probably 80 pounds less than the total weight of myself and my crew, giving them a weight advantage of about 120 pounds. The race was a long two-lap windward-leeward one, with a good steady breeze for the first lap and a half. On the last run the wind dropped rapidly and the Argentines, who had been in third place at the windward mark, caught the English boat on the run and could have passed me if the race had not ended when it did.

Special care should be taken to reduce the weight of anything that is above the water line, particularly in the mast and in the rigging. In the past most small boats had excessively heavy masts and rigging. At present, masts are aluminum and the boat builders have done a pretty good job of testing for weight and strength. You need not do much except keep up with the latest developments with an eye to saving weight.

Much consideration has been given to achieving a low moment of inertia. The goal is to concentrate as much weight as possible in the center of the boat. The weight of fittings at the bow and stern has been reduced as has the weight of masts. A boat encountering a wave will tend to pitch up and down, and resistance to this pitching increases drag and slows the boat. A low moment of inertia will make a boat turn more quickly when tacking and will make it bounce its way better through chop. Some builders have gone to extremes, to the point of reducing hull thickness at the ends and making up for it with increased thickness at the center.

The approach is correct, but if carried too far the strength and durability of the boat are vastly reduced. However, the point to keep in mind is to watch for weight buildup in the ends. Use a strong lightweight fitting in place of a heavy one and keep all fittings as close to the center as possible. Do not store the anchor, life jackets, etc. in the stern. It might not make too much difference but it could mean a few seconds per mile—and many races have been lost by just a few seconds. Several one-design classes have minimum values for moment of inertia.

The location of the hull's center of gravity is not usually considered of much consequence and is not normally controlled in a one-design class. In a recent account of a Finn-class National Championship in Australia, Ched Proctor, the winner, reported that a change in Finn-class restrictions which permitted moving some weight forward resulted in a big increase in boat speed on a beat—further proof that little things count.

Proctor also mentioned that some of the hulls had double bottoms, which allowed them to self-bail going to windward in heavy weather. This of course permitted them to arrive at the windward mark dry and to take off on a plane instantly on rounding the mark. On occasion this would result in an insurmountable lead over a boat which arrived at the mark with a large quantity of water on board.

One of the most useful tools you can have in working on boats is a pop rivet gun, available at most hardware stores. The principle is to insert the body of the rivet into the proper-size hole. The gun pulls the shaft out and collapses the body. As soon as the shaft breaks the body has been compressed enough to give a tight fit. Rivets are particularly good for installing fittings on masts and booms. I have seen a number of fittings riveted on fiberglass decks but prefer a through-bolt any time there is much of a load. For most installations, aluminum rivets are quite satisfactory. Stainless-steel rivets are available but require a heavy-duty gun. It would be well to inspect aluminum rivets a couple of times a year, particularly if you sail in salt water.

Small-boat sailing has now become a very popular sport and there are many manufacturers of fittings. In the United States, as late as the mid-1960's there were only two or three companies supplying parts. Now there are dozens and you can usually find what you need. Plastics are prevalent, and where they can be used they will save weight over aluminum. Both are easy to work in a home shop with hand tools if you need to modify them.

A home workshop is a valuable asset in sailing. It seems that every year a part or fitting needs to be replaced, or something new has developed that you must add. Many power tools are not necessary, but a small electric drill and a sabre saw are essential. A sander-polisher is also helpful. Add the usual complement of hand tools and a worktable with vise, and you can take care of just about anything that comes up, unless you are trying to build a boat from scratch.

Any projection or roughness underwater will produce drag. The slot around the centerboard should be closed as tightly as possible. Here, incidentally, is the only advantage of the dagger-type centerboard over the pivot type. With the dagger-type centerboard, a metal plate can be set into the keel to fit tightly around the board and not permit water to flow into and out of the centerboard trunk. The turbulence of this water entering and leaving the centerboard trunk will cause an appreciable amount of drag. Rubber and plastic flaps are available and work well if properly installed. They should, of course, be set into the keel (if allowed by class rules).

There are two theories on cockpit size. Prior to the development of self-bailers, such as the well-known Elvstrom Bailer, the preference was for a fairly small cockpit. This kept much of the water from entering the boat when it capsized. An agile skipper and crew could frequently right the boat without taking on any water. The small cockpit combined with large spray rails went a long way towards keeping the boat dry.

With the advent of reliable self-bailers and transom flaps, cockpits have become larger. Water entering the boat from spray or capsize is rapidly removed. Larger cockpits enable the skipper and crew to move farther out or aft and permit more effective balancing of the boat. Larger cockpits (and smaller spray rails) also help to reduce weight.

In England, they have developed very large suction bailers which they call "open door bailers." The undecked dinghys sailed over there use as many as four of these to keep the water out.

4

Centerboards and Rudders

THERE IS AN ENORMOUS AMOUNT OF TECHNICAL DATA ON THE SUBJECT OF centerboards and rudders, probably enough to fill several books. Since this is better left to the designers, I will only touch on a few technical aspects, and give some pointers that will be helpful to the average sailor.

First and foremost, the finish should be as good as you can possibly get it. Many classes specify metal centerboards, particularly aluminum, and it is fairly easy to maintain the finish. However, oxidation takes its toll, especially in salt water. As with everything else, careful handling will reduce the amount of work involved in upkeep. After every sail in salt water, the centerboard should be thoroughly rinsed in fresh water. Even this will not preserve aluminum and it should be wet sanded frequently with 400- or 600-grade paper. A little soap or detergent will make the sanding easier and help to remove the salt. Scratches and gouges should be sanded fair and any that are deep should be filled with epoxy putty. Stainless steel is the other most common metal and requires less work. In days gone by, bronze was often used, but it is too expensive now. A regular steel board is difficult to maintain because of rust, and it is essential to paint or plate a board of this material.

Next to metal, the second most used material for centerboards is fiberglass, and these boards are about equal to stainless in required maintenance. As is the case with the hull, the resin continues to cure and it is necessary to give as much care to the fiberglass centerboard as you do to the hull.

Many scratches on centerboards come from protrusions in the centerboard trunk. This is not an easy thing to cure but it can be done. You can determine the approximate location of the source of the scratches by looking at the board. Most situations call for sanding inside of the trunk. This is best accomplished with the boat on the trailer, rolled over 90 degrees. Leaving the mast in and tying it down will help stabilize the boat. Make a sanding tool by using a batten and gluing pieces of foam rubber on each side for 4 or 5 inches, the total thickness being slightly more than the width of the opening in the hull. Stick sandpaper on both sides with adhesive such as rubber cement. Then sand the inside of the trunk until the imperfection has been removed.

Most rudders are fiberglass or wood, with some being wood covered with fiberglass. Wood traditionally has been the preferred material, but now the trend is to all-fiberglass. Since fiberglass is heavy, most rudders are hollow with good buoyancy. However, any small pinhole will leak water. Many fiberglass rudders are foam filled, which eliminates this problem. Thoroughly sanding the wooden rudder is a job requiring a rubber block or just hand sanding, since no fairing is required, assuming it was fair to start with. Paint or varnish is not as hard as resin, so you will have to refinish the rudder after a number of sandings.

Modifications can be made to shapes even within class rules. For example, it is possible to have either sharp or blunt edges. Present technical data indicates that the leading edges should be rounded or elliptical and the trailing edges squared off. Even a metal centerboard can be rounded off to attain, as near as possible, the shape shown in the diagram. The trailing edge can be filed off to about $\frac{1}{16}$ inch, but be careful to make the corners sharp, without any hooks.

Usually more can be done with the shape of the rudder. The maximum thickness should be about 35 percent aft of the leading edge. How thick to make the rudder involves a compromise. A thinner rudder probably has an advantage in lighter air and inland conditions, with the thicker section better in heavier wind and bigger seas. A thickness of approximately 12 percent of the chord (blade width) would be a good compromise, using the N.A.C.A. family series of airfoils as a starting point (see Figure 1).

Close attention should be given to the method of attaching the rudder to the boat. The rudder pintles and gudgeons should be strong and firmly bolted. There is a tremendous force applied in turning the rudder in a heavy sea, so only heavy-duty types made of stainless steel should be used. I can remember one light air race when the tiller started twisting in my hand—the brass fittings had

SUGGESTED RUDDER CROSS SECTION

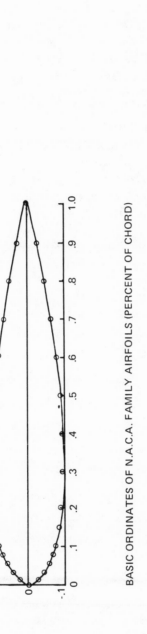

BASIC ORDINATES OF N.A.C.A. FAMILY AIRFOILS (PERCENT OF CHORD)

Sta.	0	1.25	2.5	5.0	7.5	10	15	20	25	30	40	50	60	70	80	90	95	100
Ord.	0	3.157	4.358	5.925	7.000	7.805	8.909	9.563	9.902	10.003	9.672	8.823	7.606	6.107	4.372	2.413	1.344	0.210

FIGURE 1

Reprinted from N.A.C.A. Technical Report 460

worn and the rudder just floated out. This brings up another point: always have a positive rudder lock. There is nothing more disheartening than to have righted your boat after capsize, to find that the rudder has floated off. One method is to drill a hole in the top pintle and insert a cotter pin after the rudder is in place. Spring clips and swinging lock fittings are also used.

Check the pin in the centerboard to make sure it is sound, as some have fallen out, with the resulting loss of the board. Dagger boards are much more subject to loss and I always (so far) tie mine in immediately after putting the board into the trunk. Both types should have some means of preventing the board from completely disappearing into the trunk if the boat should turn completely upside down. Righting the boat without a bit of the board sticking out for a handhold is virtually impossible.

5

Finish of the Hull

A SMOOTH SURFACE ON THE HULL IS OF THE UTMOST IMPORTANCE. ALSO, it must be absolutely fair, which means that it must not have any waves in it. One might think that those beautifully smooth fiberglass hulls could not have waves in them but they do—maybe not when brand new, but they will. The reason is that the resin continues to cure for a long time and there may be a noticeable lack of fairness during at least the first few years. The cure for this lack of fairness is sanding with wet-or-dry paper and a sanding block which conforms as closely as possible to the curvature of the hull. Surfaces with single curvature may be sanded with a wood block, but a flexible block must be used on double-curved surfaces to avoid sanding through the gelcoat.

Care must also be used in sanding near edges. Some corners must be left sharp, such as the intersection of the bottom and the transom. Number-400 paper is normally used. A bucket of warm water and some household detergent will keep the paper from clogging and will facilitate progress. Be careful not to sand too deeply. If there are any scratches, they should be filled with putty. For small scratches, lacquer-based putty such as is used in autobody shops works well. For deeper gouges, a material with an epoxy or polyester resin base will harden faster.

There are two schools of thought on what the ultimate finish should be. The older theory was a highly polished finish secured with rubbing compound and a buffer. Dirt and dust will not adhere to this type of finish but neither will water, and there is a modern theory that there is more resistance between this non-wetted surface and the water than there is between layers of water, the first layer adhering to the surface. A surface sanded with 400 paper supposedly gives the desired interface with the water molecules, and detergent used with wet sanding will remove all oiliness which is undesirable. This latter system has the advantage of easier maintenance and I accept the theory that it is superior from a performance standpoint.

If you decide to buff, fine-grade rubbing compound found in auto-parts stores is satisfactory. Borrowing or renting a heavy-duty polishing machine with a lamb's-wool bonnet will cut down the time required. Use a pie pan to mix the rubbing compound with water to form a thick paste and daub a bit on the bonnet. It is a messy job but the results are worth it.

No one who is serious about competitive racing leaves his boat in the water. A good hull finish cannot be maintained, because of various marine growths. Large cruising boats that must be left in the water require a good anti-fouling paint, but this is not practical for small boats, since the paint will absorb water and increase the weight. Wood, of course, absorbs water, and even fiberglass will pick up some. Accordingly, the boat should be stored on a trailer.

Since most sailing waters are not as clean as we would like, dirt will adhere to the bottom. This requires that you rinse and sponge off the boat every time you sail, and wash it with detergent if there happens to be oil in the water. Salt will cake on the boat if it is not rinsed with fresh water. Salt retains moisture and will pick up dust and dirt from the air.

One thing to be on the lookout for is surface blisters in fiberglass boats. They may happen when the surface maintains contact with water. The blisters are usually shallow and less than ⅛ inch in diameter, but they can be larger. There is disagreement as to the cause, but apparently water is absorbed into the surface and raises the gelcoat. Some boats are more prone to the problem than others, and although bottom paint alleviates blistering, it does not eliminate it. If you properly store your boat on a trailer you should not have this problem. However, I have seen blisters located in the area where the boat sits on the trailer. Apparently the carpeting remained wet for extended periods of time. To prevent this, use carpeting made of synthetic material since the material itself does not absorb water. It would seem that a thin loose-woven carpet would dry more rapidly.

The only cure for blisters is to sand all the way through, and leave a cavity. If the void is small, it can be touched up easily with some matching resin. Larger cavities require a fiberglass putty. In any case, take care not to have too much buildup, since you will have to re-sand. Several thin applications are better than a single thick one.

6

Masts and Booms

MASTS ARE NOW BEING CONSTRUCTED OF ALUMINUM ALMOST EXCLU-
sively. This was a trend started in the late 1950's when it became
obvious that good wood for masts was becoming rare. Some attempts have been made to use other materials. Titanium has
proven too expensive except for such boats as twelve meters.
There has been some development in fiberglass but it is too soon
to pass judgment. Aluminum has proved to be satisfactory, since
the bend characteristics of one specimen are very much like the
next. There can be some differences, in that the dies do wear, and
tapering varies. As the dies wear, the extrusion walls become
thicker and, of course, less bendy. Tapering is done by cutting and
removing a thin, pie-shaped section, and then welding the mast
back together. The problem occurs in the welding; if not welded
correctly, the mast will twist if the heat is unevenly applied. In any
case, most masts of the same model are uniform, which could
never be said about wooden masts.

The perfect mast does not exist. Ideally the mast should be
light, have a small diameter, a low center of gravity, and a minimum amount of rigging. It should be fairly flexible in medium
wind, but not enough to throw the mainsail out of shape when the
wind becomes stronger. Taking everything into consideration, the
best recommendation would be to pick the mast that has similiar
bend characteristics to the one your sailmaker uses for testing.
Most classes have one or more sailmakers competing, and they are
usually proficient sailors. They do a great amount of testing and
settle on a pattern for their sails based on the bend of the mast they

are using. This is not to say that you must use the same mast the sailmaker uses, but it does simplify the problem.

Most mast manufacturers have gone to a great deal of trouble to build their masts with the lowest center of gravity and the minimum amount of windage, so the choice is usually between a large-diameter section with thin walls, and a small-diameter section with thicker walls, the latter being the heavier one. The trend now is towards a smaller, thin-walled section, using various rigging devices to control the bend.

Weight is an important consideration. Get a mast that is as light as feasibly possible. In any conditions other than a drifter, your boat will encounter waves which tend to upset its balance, causing it to pitch back and forth. This disrupts the smooth air flow across the sails, as well as the smooth flow of water under the hull. The more weight aloft (as well as anywhere away from the pivot point), the longer the pitching will continue. This is what sailors are thinking about when they worry about the moment of inertia.

Mast stiffness is the next consideration. Since most sails are now designed for masts that bend, a very stiff mast will not produce an optimum mainsail until winds are in the upper range; most racing is done in light-to-medium conditions, so it would be a handicap to have a stiff mast. Furthermore, a bendier mast flattens the sail by removing the draft, thereby reducing the crew weight required. Obviously, the less weight you need to hold the boat flat, the faster you can go. So, the conclusion is to use a lighter, bendier mast if your crew weight is on the low side, and vice versa. This should not be carried to extremes on the bendy side either. Too much bend will "turn the sail inside out" before you get out of the medium range of winds.

Assume that you have a mast which many sailors in your class are using with success, but you feel it is either too bendy or too stiff. This is where the various mast controls become important. The most obvious of these is the adjustable backstay. Tightening the backstay pulls the top of the mast down and aft, flexing the center of the mast forward. Larger racing yachts have used hydraulic backstay adjusters with great success. Smaller boats run the backstay through a block on the stern and then forward to a tackle arrangement giving mechanical advantage. In either case you can get just about whatever bend you need. Most smaller centerboarders do not have backstays, so you have to resort to other means of control.

Most methods of attaining bend are determined by the way the boat is rigged. The first step in getting more bend is to modify the spreaders. Assuming a limited swing spreader, setting it to angle farther aft will produce more bend fore and aft. The airfoil spreader swings aft until its base touches the mast. Filing at this point will permit it to go farther aft. Be careful to remove the same amount of material on both spreaders. Determining that they are even can be accomplished by supporting the mast level on both ends. Drop a plumb bob from the bolt-rope slot and measure the tip of the spreader to the plumb-bob line. The distance from both spreaders should be the same. It is a good idea to know the distance between the ends of the spreaders; this will give you a record of what you are doing as well as a means of comparing with other skippers. If you want to reduce the angle of the spreader, block the base so it will not swing as far aft. Use almost any hard material, such as a hard plastic or metal, held up with tape. Coins can be used in a pinch.

Shrouds should have a stop where the spreader is attached. The stop should be located so that the spreader bisects the angle made by the shroud where it passes over the spreader. Without stops the spreader brackets on the mast tend to loosen, resulting in the spreader dropping at the outboard end, thus destroying the equal angles. A stop can be made out of part of a sleeve, which is crimped to the shroud. A piece of copper wire could be used. Wrap the shroud a couple of times with the copper wire and cinch it with a pair of pliers, just hard enough to embed some of the copper into the shroud.

Bending the mast while sailing can be accomplished by applying the boom vang or sheeting harder on the mainsheet. Both procedures pull the boom down, which in turn tightens the leech of the mainsail, which pulls the top of the mast aft. The problem is that in lighter winds you hook the leech of the mainsail. This should be done only when the wind is blowing hard enough to keep the leech from hooking. Also effective is arranging the main sheet so that when it leaves the boom it angles forward. This tends to thrust the boom forward and bend the mast.

If you have done all of these things, the mast should be fairly bendy. Perhaps all of the above changes would not be necessary; certainly they should not all be made at once, as it would be easy to overdo. After each change, the boat should be tested to see if you have the desired bend. If the mast bends too much, deforming the sail in the process, you need some means of preventing the mast from bending as much. Some skippers get along nicely with putting wood blocks in front of the mast at the deck level. They arrive at the thickness of the blocks by experimentation. However, the blocks can become a nuisance, particularly if you sail a loose-

rigged boat and the mast needs to go forward when on the downwind leg. There are several bend-control devices on the market,
but the best one I have seen was designed by Earl Elms of the
Snipe Class, and is known as the "Elms Puller." It is a lever arm
attached to a swivel pin which is fastened to a bolt on the back side
of the mast at deck level. The arm has two control lines, one to pull
the mast forward and one to pull the mast aft. The beauty of it is
that, by cleating both control lines, the mast is locked in place. A
skipper can install his own bend control device by using a series
of blocks to give mechanical advantage, or by using a drum installed just aft of the mast, hooking it to a bolt in the back of the
mast with an S hook.

Frequently, the slot for the luff rope is too wide for the sails you
are using. Halyards jump out of the slot when the mast bends if
they are led inside this slot. In addition to the extra windage, the
halyards tend to bend the mast beyond the point where you have
calculated it should be. A related problem is that the sail jams in
the slot at the starting point when the sail is hoisted. All of this is
easily solved with a wooden mallet or block of wood and a ham-
mer. Lay the mast on the ground, preferably a soft grassy spot, and
gently close the slot until the wire will not pull through, or the
mainsail goes up easily when hoisting. If you go too far, you can
open up the slot with a wooden wedge. Continued flexing of the
mast opens up the slot so you may have to do this procedure again.

Occasionally, a mast will take a permanent bend. It is not really permanent unless the wall is dented. Straightening the mast
can be accomplished by laying it across two padded supports,
about 8 feet apart. Center the maximum bend point between the
supports, bend side up, and get someone to hold the mast in this
position. Bounce on it several times, then sight down it to check
your progress. It takes a fair amount of force, but the process
should be gradual, thus avoiding bending it in the other direction.

As with masts, aluminum has replaced wood as the material
used for booms. Wooden booms tended to split at the bolt-rope slot,
allowing the foot to pull out. If the foot pulled out only a couple of
feet it probably did not do too much damage, but it was a tremendous psychological barrier. Aluminum solved this problem, in addition to providing a stiffer boom, and since they are hollow, a
place to put rigging control lines without increasing windage.

Some years ago, the only function of the boom was to hold the
foot of the mainsail out, and to provide a place to attach the mainsheet. No thought was given to adjusting the tension of the foot of
the sail while sailing. Life was a good deal simpler then. But someone discovered that slackening the tension on the foot put more

draft into the sail. Now we have two controls on the boom, both controlling the draft. The first control sets the amount of tension on the foot for windward work—this varies depending upon the wind strength. The other control is usually a Hyfield lever which releases tension for off-the-wind sailing.

7

Rigging the Boat

MOST BOATS WILL NOT BE PERFECTLY BALANCED UNDER ALL WIND VELO-cities; a slight lee helm with a light wind will not do any harm, but carrying the rudder deflected in a high wind to counteract weather helm will slow down the boat by an appreciable amount. Therefore, the boat should be rigged to have a slight lee helm in a light wind, if necessary, in order to reduce as much as possible the weather helm which the boat will possess in a high wind. This may generally be accomplished by locating the mast as far forward as possible and the centerboard as far back as possible. Moving the forestay back and forth has some effect on balance, but not nearly as much as the location of the mast or centerboard.

With a pivot-type centerboard, swinging the board back a little will greatly reduce weather helm, and without the center of gravity of the board being raised by an appreciable amount.

According to Manfred Curry's theories on the relative location of the jib and main, the jib stay should be as far back as possible. Dr. Curry conducted very extensive experiments on actual boats and on models of sails. He arrived at a number of conclusions, most of which I think are correct; however, there is one very unfortunate thing about the science of aerodynamics and its practical application—whether to airplanes or to sails—and that is that the air currents didn't go to college, they haven't read the books, and they don't always do what the best aerodynamic theories say they should. The aerodynamics engineers of aircraft companies have done their best to educate these air currents by using exact-scale power models in excellent wind tunnels, calculating results with slide rules, calculators, and now computers, but airflow remains illiterate—it still cannot read, and all theories must be modified by experience with the actual airplane or sailboat.

This probably sounds like rank heresy in a book on scientific sailing, but before jumping to this conclusion refer back to the definition of scientific sailboat racing in the introduction. Here is a typical case where it is necessary to be sure of your facts first, and then be sure that the conclusions at which you arrive are correct. It is also the first of numerous examples where an attempt to blindly apply principles of airplane aerodynamics to a sailboat will get you into trouble. Airplane wings and sails aren't the same —an airplane wing has two rigid surfaces, and a sail has a single flexible surface; their only similarity is that they both produce lift when the wind blows on them.

The accepted theory is that the jib and the main together work like a slotted wing on an airplane. I am convinced that the jib does not contribute anything to the efficiency of the main by the slot effect, and that its primary contribution is from the fact that it is in itself a very efficient sail without any mast to induce turbulent airflow right at the leading edge of the airfoil section. A slotted wing section produces high lift at high angles of attack, but also produces a high drag which results in a lower ratio of lift to drag with the slot open than with it closed. With a sail, we are working at as low an angle of attack as we can get, and we couldn't get a very efficient slot anyway even if we wanted it, because if we get the jib close enough to the main to accelerate the airflow the way it does with an airfoil slot, the main just collapses at the luff.

(When the paragraph above first appeared in 1950, it was not only considered heretical then—as a matter of fact it was twenty-five years before anyone showed any signs of agreeing in print. Mr. Arvel Gentry, a research aerodynamicist, conducted a sophisticated investigation into the subject of how a jib and a main actually affect each other and came to the conclusion that the generally accepted slot theory was all wrong, reporting his conclusions in a series of articles in *Sail* magazine. I was not really worried but I feel better now.)

A forward rake on the mast will help to counteract weather helm, but the sails will set better in a light wind if the mast is raked slightly aft. The roach on the leech of the mainsail has a tendency to fall over in light air anyway, and any forward rake of the mast tends to make this worse. By raking the mast aft, the entire luff of the sail is supported by the bolt rope—not just hung from the headboard.

It is desirable to have the shrouds far away from the mast in order to cut down the compression load in the mast. The current practice of sheeting to a very close angle eliminates the question of whether to run sheets outside the shrouds; run them inside. This does prevent the jib from going outboard of the shroud when on a reach, but the advantage of better performance to windward more than offsets the slight disadvantage in reaching.

Where there is a choice of deck-stepped or keel-stepped mast, the latter is advisable. Obviously, the keel-stepped mast is longer and more bend can be induced. However, the biggest advantage is that the bend can be partially controlled through a system of blocks or levers. The only advantage of a deck-stepped mast is you don't lose it if a shroud breaks. If this occurs with a keel-stepped mast it invariably breaks or bends so badly it cannot be fixed. Stepping the mast on the keel means that the hole in the deck will limit the amount that the mast can move sideways. It should have clearance fore and aft so the mast can bend. The sides of the hole should have a lining that can be replaced when it begins to wear. A couple of strips of plywood held by screws on each side should be sufficient. Teflon strips are better.

When the boat is sailing, the stay on the windward side is automatically tight, and the stay on the leeward side is automatically loose. The luff of the jib and the forestay are kept tight when on a beat by the pull from the mainsheet being transferred from the boom to the mainsail. As the boat goes from a beat to a reach and still farther out of the wind to a run, the load on the jib stay becomes progressively less. This is a disadvantage and on a reach, the mast should be blocked back, a mast aft puller should be used, or the jib halyard should be tightened. Until recently, blocks or the mast puller have generally been used; however, with the new light bendy masts, the jib halyard may be the answer. With the whisker pole out, the slack luff is an advantage.

The exact amount of slack in the shrouds does not seem to be important, but they should be much looser than one would think —particularly for a skipper accustomed to larger boats. However, various boats require different tension. It depends on the design as well as the current fashion. Over the course of 40 years, the Snipe class has gone to tight rigging, to very loose rigging (the masts looked as if they would jump out of the boat at the first opportunity), and now to a more moderate rigging but still not tight. As with anything else, it is a trade-off. With loose rigging, the mast can go forward on a downwind run, making a noticeable difference in speed. However, tighter rigging increases pointing ability. Since most race courses favor windward work, the tighter rigging should be chosen rather than very loose rigging.

Standing rigging is rather simple. You choose the wire with the greatest breaking strength for the size you need. In stainless, this is 1×19 construction. It is not very flexible but you do not need much flexibility for the stays and shrouds. In addition, it is the cheapest of the three varieties usually available from marine supply stores. There is no question that swaged terminals are best for standing rigging. Use aircraft eyes rather than marine eyes since they are just as good and cheaper in the sizes most frequently used in small boats. Eyes are used when the top is attached inside the mast and the other end is attached to a stay adjuster. If attaching to mast tangs and chain plates, a fork end is used.

The big drawback in using stainless-steel swaged terminals is the cost and unavailability of a swaging service. My own fleet has the use of an army surplus hand-swaging machine. It produces a mechanical advantage of 400 to 1, which is enough to squeeze the terminal end metal into all the voids of the wire, thus becoming a solid piece of metal. I have never seen one of these terminals fail, but the wire will break near the terminal, particularly if salt water is allowed to accumulate at that point. If you do not have a swaging machine available locally, most marine or aircraft supply stores can do swaging for you. You have to give them exact lengths, which is not easy if you are rigging a new mast and do not have an old shroud or forestay to measure.

Terminals can be made using copper sleeves and thimbles. Run the wire through one side of the sleeve, around the thimble, and back through the sleeve. Crimping can be done with a variety of tools, some inexpensive enough for everyone to have in his toolbox. According to the manufacturers of the sleeves, this arrangement is capable of supporting a greater load than the rated breaking strength of the wire. I have seen these terminals on boats that have been through a lot of heavy weather, so I guess the claims are valid. The big advantage of these terminals is cost, plus the fact that any sailor can install them. The big disadvantage is more windage, and since they are larger, they are more difficult to attach to the mast. The dissimilar metals could cause trouble.

The only other terminal fittings that seem practical are the Norseman type. They can be attached with a wrench and are not really complicated. They are a little bulky but could be used in an emergency. Half of the fitting is threaded into the other half and spreads the wire with a cone in the core of the wire. However, I have a large distaste for any fitting that could come unscrewed. On two occasions I have been on boats when a turnbuckle came loose. Both were of the tubular type with a check nut locking system. Obviously, the nut did not lock it.

Stays, and shrouds should have some means of adjusting their length. It would be nice to have the lengths predetermined for maximum boat speed. However, someone always comes up with a different method of tuning for a particular suit of sails and off we go. In addition, there are different styles of sailing, different crew weights, and even different boats. For example, in one-design classes boats are always a little different. None has the weight distributed exactly like the next one. Besides, when a skipper adds his own choice of equipment, the boat will be different. So, provide for a method of adjusting the standing rigging.

Since I have already stated my aversion for turnbuckles, I can only offer an item known as a stay adjuster. This is merely a small piece of channel 4 to 5 inches in length with 10 to 12 holes. The terminal is inserted inside the channel and secured with a clevis pin. This will provide all the ajustment you could want.

Halyards present a bit more problem than standing rigging. The difference is that halyards must go around a sheave. Use 7 × 19 construction for halyards; this is the most flexible. In order to save weight aloft, sheaves are made as light and small as possible. This limits the size of the wire that can be used since the sheave diameter can be reduced only to a certain point before the wire will fail. Smaller wire helps in reducing the weight aloft. Usually two or three sizes are practical on a given mast; I would recommend use of the smallest size, moving up one size if the wire starts to fail before you feel you have gotten proper service. The latter is difficult to describe; if you sail in light winds the smaller size will suffice, but if you sail in heavy winds and seas, a larger size will be necessary.

One skipper has recommended replacing all wire at least every two years. He usually sails in heavy weather and drives his boat very hard. If he combines this with the salt-water atmosphere, he probably gets full use from his wire. If you decide to adopt this sort of schedule, it might pay to use galvanized wire. This sounds like rank heresy in the day of strong, lightweight stainless but it has some points. Galvanized wire, for a given size, has a greater breaking strength than stainless and gives you warning when it is about to break—by getting rusty. Stainless wire sometimes breaks even after you have just inspected it.

All wire should be inspected at every opportunity. Some do this by running their hands the full length of the wire in both directions. A better method is to use a piece of cloth, as it will catch a stray strand and is easier on the hands. I have heard that you can tuck one stray strand back and not worry but I prefer to replace it at the first sign of wear. The most frequent point of failure is where the wire goes around the sheave, particularly if the sheave does not fit closely to the mast and the wire slips off. You will know when this occurs as the halyard will resemble a long corkscrew. Any breaks at this point will call for a complete new wire. The other failure point is at the end which attaches to the sail by means of a shackle. This gets a lot of wear but you can usually fit another terminal without losing more than half an inch of wire. Of course this requires making an adjustment for the connection at the other end.

By far the best means of attaching the halyard to the sail is to use a strap shackle with a captive pin and a hole at the other end. Thread the halyard through the hole and put on a swaged ball or crimped sleeve stop. The other end of the main halyard should be secured to a hook. Locate the hook on the back of the mast at deck level. This arrangement is more secure than using a cleat. The other end of the jib halyard should be secured to a lever or drum, which enables you to adjust the tension while sailing.

The Cunningham hole was named for Briggs Cunningham, skipper of the twelve meter that won the Americas' Cup in 1958. This development has probably done as much to enable adjustment of sails as any other single item. It is a grommet in the mainsail just aft of the luff and 6 to 8 inches above the foot. Attach one end of a line to the mast, then run it through the hole and down to a cleat and you have the basic rig. Pull the line at the cleat end and you tighten the luff of the sail. Use a couple of blocks to gain mechanical advantage and you can easily adjust it while sailing.

The jib Cunningham performs the same function as the one for the mainsail. The best way to rig this is to have a light wire running through a block in the deck just aft of the tack of the jib and back to a cleat under the deck. A straight line pull is sufficient for small boats, but a two-or three-part purchase can easily be rigged. A simple rig can be made by drilling a hole in the tack fitting on the deck and inserting a small piece of copper tubing, flared at the top. Run the wire down through the tubing back to the cockpit and pull. The tubing will bend to the proper shape and, although there is more friction than with a block, it will serve adequately. I have used such an arrangement on my boat for a number of years.

Some method of adjusting the tension of the foot of the mainsail should be provided. Years ago the only method was to have a piece of line at the clew which was secured to a cleat on the end of the boom, but this prevented adjustment while sailing. The simplest arrangement is to have a wire with a shackle on one end. The shackle is attached to the grommet at the clew. The wire runs around a sheave in the end of the boom and then forward to a winch or cleat which the crew can adjust. Hollow booms permit the wire to be run inside, reducing windage and eliminating the possibility of the wire snagging on something. A good variation is to attach a small block on the forward end of the wire. A separate wire runs through the block; one end goes to a cleat and the other goes to a Hyfield lever. This permits setting proper tension for windward work at the end that goes to the cleat. Throwing off the Hyfield lever lets the clew go forward a couple of inches and provides the needed draft in the sail for off-wind sailing.

All sheets should be made of braided dacron, which has the least stretch of any material. Twisted dacron can be used, but it has somewhat more stretch than the braided type and is not as flexible. The braid is certainly easier on the hands. Nylon should be used only for an anchor rode, for which it is superior since it does have more stretch. Use the smallest size that can be handled easily for various control lines. In most cases, ¼ inch is adequate for small boats. Sheets should be larger since they are constantly being handled. I have used $5/16$-inch line most of the time but it is surprising how much easier $3/8$-inch is to handle. Braid is available in various colors and this is a great help in spotting which line is which. The all-white line can look like a plate of spaghetti in the bottom of a boat.

8

Boat Equipment

FORE-AND-AFT ADJUSTMENT SHOULD BE PROVIDED FOR JIB-SHEET FAIR-leads. On smaller boats this is accomplised by having an adjustable fairlead on a track that is 12 to 15 inches long. As the boats increase in size it is best to use a block to reduce friction. This is attached to a genoa slide with a pin to secure it at the desired point. The length of the track will also increase, especially if you have genoas of different sizes. Many classes are now using a cam cleat incorporated into the fairlead. This certainly reduces the clutter in the cockpit but is not without faults. The lines can jam under the fitting or get wrapped around it. And sometimes it is difficult to uncleat the sheet fast enough to avoid a capsize.

The location of the track has been subject to much experimentation in recent years. It used to be that most boats had tracks located to give about a 15-degree angle between the jib tack and the fairlead location. Now many boats are set up for as little as a 9-degree angle. This improves pointing ability but tends to backwind the mainsail more. As a consequence sailmakers got busy and built more twist into the jibs. This resulted in the top part of the jib being farther away from the main, thereby having the advantage of pointing higher but without the disadvantage of backwinding the mainsail. I am quite sure that most sails are being built in this manner, which means that provision must be made to sheet at a closer angle.

The big problem is that the closer angle is good for light-to-medium winds and fairly smooth water. As soon as you get into heavy winds and seas you need to increase the angle. This will facilitate footing and reduce stalling when hitting waves, so it is a good idea to have a second set of tracks farther outboard to increase the angle. This does tend to clutter up the deck but, even worse, necessitates rerigging the fairleads. Psychologically, it is difficult to do this during a race, so the fairlead is usually left on the track that was used when the race started. Happily, there is an alternative—a Barber hauler. This is a method of putting the jib sheet lead farther outboard and was used on Snipes many years before the Barber twins popularized it. It is a simple arrangement where the jib sheet runs through a light block between the clew of the jib and the fairlead. The block is attached to a line that runs through a through-deck fitting, down to a cleat under the deck. The through-deck fitting is located as far outboard as possible. By tightening the line, the jib sheet is pulled outboard and serves the same purpose as another track, or several tracks for that matter.

Where to locate the through-deck fitting is another point of compromise. The Barber hauler was originally designed to put the jib lead outboard when on a reach and was located forward of the normal fairlead, but this was in the days before the close-angled jib leads. In order to use this device for windward work, it should be aft of the normal fairlead. It would not be impossible to rig two Barber haulers on each side, one for reaching and one for windward work, but this seems a bit much for boats that are now overloaded with control lines. My preference would be to have one located directly outboard of the normal fairlead. It would not be optimum, but would certainly be better than not having any adjustment.

My recommendation for track location would be 10 degrees for the normal setting and 14 to 15 degrees for heavier weather. This is, of course, for windward work. For reaching, the lead should be out as far as possible. The following table gives you the method of locating these points. Measure down the centerline of the boat to a point 7 feet aft of the jib tack. From this point measure outboard at a 90-degree angle, to the distances shown in the table for the various angles. If you are using a Barber hauler, putting a mark on the deck or Barber hauler line will indicate the outboard angle you need.

Degrees	Inches
9	13.3
10	14.8
11	16.3
12	17.9
13	19.4
14	20.9
15	22.5
16	24.1

The tracks should be bolted into a reinforcement, such as ¼-inch plywood below the deck, and tied in to the deck beams in the case of a wooden boat. Since fiberglass boats usually have supporting stringers, the plywood should be sufficient. In a high wind there is a lot of load on the fairlead, and if the track pulls out, the crew generally goes overboard and you have to fish him out, in addition to fixing the track, before you finish the race.

Free-running blocks should be provided for all sheets as well as for all other uses. Since the development of extremely lightweight roller bearing blocks, there is not much excuse for not using them. The only exception would be on larger boats where these blocks would not stand up under the loads. Harken was the first to develop these blocks and has continued to update the designs. Other manufacturers have followed suit and now there is a wide choice.

Cam-action cleats are the preferred method for holding most lines. There has been a lot of improvement in boating hardware in recent years, and this is one place that has benefited. Aluminum, stainless steel, and a variety of plastics have been used to make cam cleats. An aluminum cleat weighting 2 ounces has the same holding power as an old bronze cleat that weighed 9 ounces. The advantage of this type cleat is it can be cleated and uncleated in an instant. All cleats should be located where they can be reached easily at the time when they are needed most—which is on a beat in a high wind. Particularly important is the location of the cleat for the jib sheet—the crew should be able to cleat and uncleat easily while hiked out. There are three basic locations for jib cleats, the first being incorporated into the fairlead. If your boat has a barney post (a post attached to the aft end of the trunk) this would be my preference for locating them. The other location would be on the deck opposite the side of the fairlead. This makes it convenient for the crew when hiking out, but is a bit awkward in drifters when the crew is sitting in the bottom of the boat.

The best arrangement for the mainsheet jam cleat is on a swivel bracket that incorporates a turning block. This can be put on the back of the centerboard trunk, barney post, floorboard, or on a traveler bar running across the cockpit. This gives you access whether you are hiked out or sitting in the bottom of the boat, and permits the crew to help trim the mainsheet when rounding a mark off a run onto a beat. Many prefer to locate a block on the floorboards, running the sheet to a cleat on either side of the cockpit. This does not permit leaving the mainsheet cleated while tacking as does the other method. If you fail to uncleat while tacking it could result in a capsize while trying to reach across the cockpit to retrieve it. I used a cleat on the boom for many years and found it simple and easy to use. It is a bit difficult to use on a reach or run and, although it gives the skipper a better means of support when hiking out in a high wind, it tends to pull the boom in fairly far. Furthermore, it does not aid in bending the mast when you need it, so I no longer use this method.

A good means of bailing the boat is essential even on a small lake. You can take on lots of water in a high wind, and on larger bodies of water you need the bailing equipment even at much lower wind velocities. If you used a bucket or a hand pump as was the case some years ago, you would be handicapping yourself. Self-bailers, which can be opened while racing, can drain out a lot of water in a very short time. The most popular is the one designed by Paul Elvstrom, which comes in various sizes. It has a flap which acts as a check valve and prevents water from coming back into the boat and bails efficiently going to windward. However, this type of bailer doesn't do much to rid a whole boat full of water which results from a capsize. This problem is remedied by having transom flaps or merely holes in the transom. Either method permits some small amount of water to come in, but one has to expect a bit of water in a racing boat.

The tiller should be long enough so that the skipper can sit well forward. This should not be carried to extremes, however. One of the Snipes I sailed in the World's Championships in 1949 had a tiller that was so long that I couldn't get in front of it without sitting on my crew's lap—I had to duck under. On one occasion I finished coming about with the tiller, mainsheet, and jib sheet all wrapped around my neck. Fortunately, I got myself untangled without capsizing or hitting anything. The length should not be so long that the skipper cannot move across the cockpit without tripping over it. The tiller should also have a swiveling extension or hiking stick. It should be long enough for the skipper to control the tiller while he is hiked out, and this would depend on the beam of the boat. There are a number of manufacturers and many models have adjustable lengths.

If your class does not allow spinnakers, you should have a whisker pole which permits the jib to be trimmed out on the side opposite the mainsail on broad reaches and runs. The pole should be long enough so that when it is set, the jib is practically straight across the boat. Clips or a pin which goes through a loop at the clew of the jib can be used, but the best method is to use a fitting with a latch. They are much easier to attach and release and hold securely when jibing. The release line should be attached to the pole about halfway back, with enough slack to get hold of it easily, but not so much that it will hang up on something. The inner end should merely rest against the mast with a stop to prevent it from sliding down—too much time is lost, especially in high winds, with any arrangement which requires hooking this end of the pole into a fitting on the mast. A good stop can be made by wrapping several strips of inner tube around the mast and tying it. Incidentally, inner-tube strips can be used to tie shrouds and halyards to the mast while trailing—tape leaves a sticky residue on the mast, especially in hot weather.

A sliding fitting should be provided on a track on the front of the mast for the spinnaker pole to clip into, and a latch fitting should be provided on both ends of the pole. Proper trimming of a spinnaker requires that the height be adjustable, hence the necessity for a latch on the mast end of the pole, and both pole ends should be the same, so the spinnaker can be jibed end-for-end. Some boats are set up with control lines for raising and lowering the spinnaker pole slide. This arrangement permits adjusting the height of the pole without the crew going forward.

A gadget should be used to hold the boom down when on a reach or a run, except in very light winds. Even then, this gadget will be desirable if the sea is choppy, or if there are power boats running around, in order to prevent the boom from banging around and shaking the sails. This gadget is called a boom vang. It should lead to a point on the mast or the deck at the intersection of the mast with the deck, rather than straight down from the boom to the deck. A series of blocks giving a three- or four-part purchase will be needed if the mainsail is big and ease of adjustment is desired. On cruiser racers the boom vang is frequently rigged straight down to the deck. It has to be detached every time you jibe but has the advantage of reducing the load, which can be quite heavy.

A simple and efficient boom vang for a small boat can consist of a double block on the end of a piece of $\frac{1}{16}$-inch or $\frac{3}{32}$-inch flexible cable which attaches to the boom 2 or 3 feet back of the mast. There is a double block and becket attached to the mast at the deck. A $\frac{1}{4}$-inch or $\frac{5}{16}$-inch dacron line makes a four-part system, with the free end leading below deck and aft to a cam cleat located so it is easily accessible to the skipper or crew.

There is a retracting system to get the vang out of the way when it is not in use. This consists of a piece of $\frac{3}{16}$-inch or $\frac{1}{4}$-inch shock cord, one end of which is attached to the boom near where the vang wire attaches. It goes forward through a block at the front of the boom and terminates at a block on the wire running from the double block on the vang to the boom. With no tension on the vang, the shock cord pulls the parts of the vang up to the block at the front of the boom.

You can leave the vang on all the way around the course if you wish, except in a very light wind when it might tighten the leach too much when going to windward. Even a moderate amount of mast bend on a beat makes it ineffective but, by being left on, there is one less thing to remember as you reach the windward mark before the off-wind leg. If the crew is facing aft when coming about, the vang really does not get in the way tacking. I always leave the boom vang on when jibing even in a fairly light breeze, as it prevents "goose wing" jibes where the top of the sail stays on one tack and the rest of the sail goes on the other. When this happens you usually have a batten or two broken or lost, and may also have a ripped mainsail.

If you sail with loose shrouds, an extremely handy gadget to use in a very light wind when there is a heavy chop or there are lots of water skiers around is a piece of light line to tie between the mast and the leeward shroud. This will greatly reduce the shaking of the sails and is a big help to your peace of mind, even if it didn't help keep your boat going—which it does.

It is possible to sail a boat with the aft end of the mainsheet attached to the boat at a fixed point—but not if you want to have much control over the mainsail. This is where a traveler is needed. A traveler enables you to control the angle of the boom to the centerline of the boat without any sheet adjustment. The traditional location for a traveler is on the deck just under the end of the boom. This location has lesser loads, permitting lighter rigging as compared to a traveler located in the center of the boat. The center traveler does operate over a wider angle, but since the traveler is used mostly for windward work the aft traveler is sufficient. The exception to this is for boats with high-aspect rigs and shorter booms, particularly in racer cruisers.

Most travelers consist of a bar with a slide or car that runs athwartship. The car is usually equipped with ball bearings and control lines so that the car can be positioned at any point on the bar. The advantage of this type of traveler, when located in the center, is that the skipper can promote planing by pumping the traveler, leaving the mainsheet cleated.

An alternative is a rope traveler as used on Lasers and Snipes. This arrangement provides most of the advantages of the bar type but is less expensive and much lighter. One type consists of an adjustable bridle on which a free block rides. Another block is attached to the free block and the mainsheet runs through the second block. To keep the boom close to the centerline, the length of the bridle is increased until the blocks almost touch the boom. As the wind picks up, the length of the bridle is shortened until the free block runs as far out to leeward as is needed. The rigging of this is simple and consists of the traveler being fixed at one end, with the other end going through the deck to a turning block and then to a cleat. Shortening the bridle requires releasing the mainsheet for about a foot, but if the traveler cleat is readily accessible, the main will luff for only a second or so.

A disadvantage of this type of traveler is that in light winds, there is too much tension on the leach and not enough twist in the main. The apparent wind is much closer to parallel to the boat centerline down low than it is higher up. If the boom is pulled down tightly in a light wind, the sail is meeting the apparent wind at too high an angle of attack throughout most of its height if the boom is trimmed properly for the lower part of the sail. To remedy this situation, a sort of auxiliary traveler is necessary to take over in light winds. Generally a pair of light lines (sometimes called "pinching strings") is attached to the block on the traveler, one being led to each side of the boat terminating at a cleat or hook at a location where they can be released easily.

In light winds, the regular traveler is slacked off and the "pinching strings" are rigged so that the block is on the centerline of the boat and, at its highest distance above the deck, is about 8 to 12 inches below the boom. With this rig, the boom may be trimmed in as far as desired without removing the twist in the main. In fact, it is easy to trim it in too far, especially in a drifter. The proper amount will vary with different boats, but about halfway between the sheer and the centerline is a good place to start. When the wind picks up to the point where hiking out is necessary, this rig should be released and the regular traveler used.

A variation on the rope traveler is to use a line of fixed length with a fixed block instead of a free block. The traveler is endless and rotates around under the deck by means of through-deck blocks. A control line is attached to the traveler at the center opposite the fixed block. When the control line is cleated, the traveler cannot rotate, thus the fixed block is held to the centerline. When the control line is completely released, the boom goes all the way out. The big advantage this has is when the wind picks up you release the control line. This is easier than the other method which requires releasing the "pinching strings" and pulling in on the other traveler. There are two disadvantages to this system: sometimes it does not travel as freely as it should, and in very high winds the block cannot be pulled down as close to the deck as desired.

Hiking straps, securely fastened and properly placed, are essential. Straps break or their fastenings pull out more often than they should. I suspect most skippers do not recognize the loads involved and do not pay sufficient attention to the fastenings. Through bolting is ideal but not feasible unless the manufacturer has installed an eye bolt during the building. However, an eye bolt or strap can be bolted to a block of wood which is then fiberglassed to the bottom of the boat. Most hiking straps are run fore and aft, but some prefer to run them athwartship. The latter method permits getting out farther but severely restricts the fore-and-aft movement. Hiking straps need to be adjustable but not necessarily while racing. A skipper can establish the proper length and leave it, but to find that point some provision has to be made for adjustment. It seems that every crew is a different size and unless you have a permanent one (very rare) some adjustment is needed for his straps.

The most popular method is fore and aft, using 2-inch nylon webbing. The webbing has a grommet in one end and is about a foot short of the distance needed. A piece of line through the grommet is tied to the aft eye bolt. Varying the length of the line adjusts the length of the hiking strap. Closed-cell foam air-conditioning insulation over ⅜-inch line may substitute for webbing. The strap is supported by a length of light shock cord. Tripping is less likely, since the shock cord gives when you step on it.

A thorough inspection should be made for frayed lines or cables, loose nuts or screws, broken cotter pins, and for the proper functioning of all cleats, bailing equipment, and stopwatches. It is an excellent idea to have a ditty bag and to carry pliers, screwdriver, knife, a piece of wire, some small line, and spare tell-tale material. Bailing wire repairs should not be necessary, but they sometimes are. Battens occasionally pop out while milling around before the start, particularly in a high wind. Have an extra set in the boat.

9

The Sails

SINCE THE SAILS ARE YOUR ONLY MEANS OF PROPULSION, THEY ARE OBVI-ously of vital importance. If you are going to race seriously, there is no point in trying to save money by buying cheap sails. My recommendation is to find out which sailmakers are campaigning in your class, or at least whose sails are doing well in your class. Sailmaking is still somewhat of an art and a ⅛-inch variation in a seam here or there could make a big difference. I know of an instance when a sailor ordered a suit of Snipe sails from one of the world's topnotch sailmakers. He could not get out of his own way with them and practically gave them away. The point is not that the sailmaker was not good, he just had no experience in making Snipe sails. So find a sailmaker with some experience in your class.

In the good (?) old days of cotton, one expected a good suit of sails to last many years. I had a suit which I used in about everything from 1941 until synthetics retired them in 1954. They were getting pretty thin and the last few years I used them, I was more careful about getting caught in a good blow with them, but they went just as well as when they were new. In fact, I think they went better. They won two World Championships, three United States championships, and one Western Hemisphere Championship for me, and in the championships that I didn't win, it was never the fault of the sails.

Now the theory is, a new jib every year and a new mainsail every other year, unless you campaign pretty hard, in which case you need sails more often. It has gotten to the point where the hard campaigners end up getting two, three, or even four new suits per year. I am not so sure that it isn't good salesmanship on the part of the sailmakers. Certainly that is a part of it—after all, they have to make a living too. And affluence has had its effect also. But the real reason sails do not last is that the coating put on the cloth eventually breaks down. Cotton had no coating so had no part in this. Any woven cloth will stretch and, to reduce the stretch in dacron cloth, manufacturers have devised a method of impregnating the cloth with a resin. The finish reduces the porosity as well as the stretch, both of which improve sail performance. However, they contribute to the perishability of the sail.

One point on having a number of suits of sails is, you never get to know one suit, if you continually swap around. No two suits of sails are exactly alike. In the first place, every bolt of cloth is slightly different in the amount of stretch. Patterns are different among sailmakers, and even one sailmaker changes his pattern from time to time. And a pattern good for one weight of cloth just might not be as good for another weight. About the only way to get sails just alike is to order two suits at the same time from the same sailmaker. Just about no one does that; if the sails are not good, you have doubled your loss. My recommendation is a jib a year, and a mainsail every other year, unless you are sailing hard and in strong winds, then two jibs and one mainsail a year.

One advantage dacron sails and bendier masts have is that the average sailor can get by with one suit of all-weather sails. In the days of cotton you had to have at least a light wind suit and a heavy wind suit, and sometimes sails for three conditions. All-weather sails are a great advantage for the average skipper, as he never has to worry about having the wrong sails up. If you and your crew are very light it is possible to have your sailmaker build you a suit for your weight. However, he probably does not have too much experience with the sail and you are better off with his standard sail, and inducing more bend in the mast.

Your boat should never be left at the dock with the sails up when there is an appreciable amount of wind. Allowing the sails to flap around in this way is bound to produce a loose leech and generally shake the sails out of shape. Drop your sails if you will be tied up more than just a minute or so.

I always fold my sails carefully and put them in a bag after drying them, even if I am going to use them the next day. Also, I fold them so that all sharp folds (and therefore the resulting wrinkles) are parallel to the foot of the sail; this is the way sails are usually folded when you received them from the sailmaker. It may be silly to worry about the effect of a few wrinkles in the sail, but in my opinion this is just another one of those things which in themselves may have no measurable effect on the speed of a boat, but when many are combined may give you that 1 or 2 seconds a mile that you may need so badly.

Exposure to ultraviolet rays damages both dacron and nylon, so don't leave your sails spread out on the lawn any longer than is necessary to dry. Salt does not harm the cloth, except to increase the weight. Salt attracts moisture, which further increases the weight, and dampness does tend to stretch nylon. So hose the sails down after sailing on salt water and lay them out on the lawn to dry before putting them away. Extreme heat harms the sails, so take care not to leave them in your car trunk on a hot day.

Sails can be handwashed with a mild soap, but cloth manufacturers warn they must be thoroughly rinsed, for any residue of soap or detergent is harmful. My recommendation is to be very careful about keeping the sails clean, and never wash them, except to rinse them occasionally in fresh water.

PART II

Getting the Most Out of
Your Boat and Sails

The Shape of Speed

THE *Shape of Speed* IS THE TITLE OF A MOVIE PRODUCED BY NORTH SAILS, an apt description of just what a sailor is trying to achieve with his sails. Research has been done to establish just what shapes and angles are the best. Much of it was done in wind tunnels with rigid forms, but the results have been proven in actual practice.

Theoretically, a sail is built for one specific range of wind strength. There is an ideal amount of draft (curvature of the sail), and it is located at a specific point. Since the sail is not rigid, the shape will change when the wind increases. This is caused by the stretch of the cloth, as more pressure is applied by the wind. Not only does the draft increase, but it will move aft. When this happens, the sail shape is no longer ideal. Therefore, an attempt is made to keep the correct amount of draft, and at the proper location. This is done through various controls.

The goal is to have a minimum number of sails, and to be able to adjust the shape over as wide a range of wind velocities as possible. In small-boat racing, we are talking about one or, at most, two suits of sails. In many ways the goal is easier to achieve in small boats than in cruising boats, simply because of the sizes involved, and the fact that small-boat masts are more flexible.

Controlling draft is done by adjusting the tension on the three edges of the sail; the luff, the foot, and the leech. Tightening the luff or the foot stretches the cloth and consequently pulls cloth from the center of the sail, thus reducing the draft.

Tension on the luff controls the fore-and-aft location of the draft. As a general rule the maximum draft when sailing to windward should be 33 to 40 percent aft of the luff, although on boats with a large genoa overlap, the draft is farther aft. Suppose you are sailing to windward in 8 knots of wind, and the main is set properly. If the wind increases to 12 knots, the location of the maximum draft will move aft and the draft will increase. Applying tension on the luff will bring the draft forward, at the same time the amount of draft will be reduced.

One control for adjusting tension is a down haul on the boom —that is, adjusting the height of the boom downward for more tension and vice versa. This is sometimes difficult to manage. Most classes have bands on the mast to limit length. Sailmakers design mainsails to reach the full distance, so it is difficult to adjust tension without going beyond the bands. An alternative, and much more easily operated, is the Cunningham hole rig. Tightening the Cunningham line induces tension on the luff as effectively as a downhaul rig. One thing that must be kept in mind is that wind is constantly changing force, most of the time. This means that the Cunningham must be adjusted frequently. For this reason it must be readily available and easily operated. Knowing how much tension to apply is a matter of experience and feel, but there are two basics to keep in mind. If there is too much tension a vertical wrinkle will appear just aft of the mast. Too little tension will cause horizontal wrinkles just aft of the mast.

Tension on the foot controls the amount of draft in the lower half of the sail. Increasing the tension reduces the draft and, incidentally, lowers the heeling moment by lowering the draft. The control for this is the clew outhaul. Here again most mainsails are designed to go all the way out to the band in medium winds of about 15 to 18 knots. There is not much you can do to increase tension for winds above that, but tension can be reduced for lighter winds. In off-wind sailing, releasing the Hyfield lever will provide more draft and increased power.

There are two basic controls for the leech: the sheet and the boom vang. Too little tension results in what is known as a loose leech. This means the cloth in the leech area becomes flat and drive is lost. In an extreme case, the leech becomes very flat and flaps like a flag. In this situation the leech has been stretched and distorted, but it does illustrate the point. This flapping is called "motor boating." Inadequate tension on the leech means draft in the aft section of the sail has been reduced. Moreover, it has allowed the maximum point of the draft to move forward which reduces its effectiveness. Too much tension increases the draft in the aft part, and curves the leech to windward. This is known as a hooked leech. An extremely hooked leech will present a flat surface at a large angle to the wind, and act like a brake. Tightening the mainsheet increases the tension and is the primary control for windward work. Off the wind where the boom is not over the traveler, and the mainsheet is no longer pulling down, the boom vang is the primary control.

A secondary control for leech tension is a leech line (prohibited in some classes). This is a small piece of line running inside the tabling on the leech and attached at the head, with the adjustment end at the clew. Pulling in this line tightens the leech and is most effective in light air when little tension is desired on the mainsheet or boom vang. Care must be taken not to apply so much tension that it hooks the leech.

Mast bend affects draft in the mainsail by reducing draft in the forward part of the sail. As the mast bends, cloth is pulled forward, causing the maximum draft to move aft. More tension on the Cunningham will be necessary to pull the draft back forward. Bend is more pronounced in smaller boats and with jib-head rigs. Sails are built with a luff curve which helps put draft in the sail in the first place. The amount of curve depends on the flexibility of the mast. For this reason, the sailmaker needs to know the bend characteristics of the mast before he can make a good sail. Sails are built to accommodate a certain amount of bend, and when the mast bends beyond that point it is necessary to use the bend control to prevent further bending. It is usually easy to tell when the mast has bent too far. Wrinkles radiate from the clew towards the mast, and since draft has been removed from the forward part of the sail, it is flat behind the mast. Furthermore, the weather helm will increase greatly.

Most of the previous discussion has been directed towards the mainsail. However, the same principles apply to the jib or genoa. The main difference is that only one line controls the foot and leech tensions—this line is the jib sheet. Trimming the sheet in applies tension to both the foot and the leech at the same time. Additional tension can be applied to one without reducing the tension on the other by moving the fairlead. If you move the fairlead forward, leech tension is increased and foot tension is decreased. This is the same as loosening the outhaul on the mainsail and tightening the mainsheet, both of which induce more draft in the sail. Moving the fairlead aft reduces tension on the leech and increases it on the foot, thus flattening the sail. Leech lines can be used in jibs the same as in mainsails. Some attempt has been made to use a foot line, thus permitting adjustment on the foot. It must be remembered that leech and foot lines are strictly secondary controls and their use is prohibited in some classes.

Control of the draft in the luff of the jib is done by tension on the halyard and on the Cunningham. Generally, the jib is hoisted with appropriate tension on the halyard for the force of the wind. The Cunningham is used for the finer adjustments. Both should be easily adjusted while racing and this means mechanical advantage is needed, particularly with the halyard. Some smaller boats have rigs to adjust the tension from the tack end of the halyard by running a control line under the deck to the cockpit. The amount of tension that can be applied by this method is limited unless the jib is hoisted some distance above the deck. This tends to reduce the decksweeper effect, which means the wind escapes under the foot of the jib. With the jib close to the deck, wind is contained in the sail, providing more drive. It seems to make more sense to adjust the halyard from the other end.

As the wind increases there is more force on the jib, and consequently on the forestay to which the jib is attached. Since the forestay is not rigid, it sags aft and to leeward, and this induces more draft into the jib. The way to control sag is to tighten the backstay. In a small boat with no backstay, the only way to control sag is increased tension on the mainsheet.

Draft control up to this point has been discussed in terms of sailing to windward, because this is the point of sailing where aerodynamic flow is the primary driving force. As you sail farther off the wind this becomes less a factor, and is minor when the wind is aft of beam. The principal driving force then becomes the sail's resistance to the wind. Wind pressures are reduced and result in less cloth stretch. Since a curved surface offers more resistance than a flat one, edge tensions should be reduced by easing the clew outhaul and the Cunningham. Be careful not to overdo this as the total surface presented to the wind will be reduced. This is the reason for using the boom vang; without it the boom will rise up and drastically decrease the area.

As the height above water increases, the true-wind velocity increases, and since the boat speed remains constant, the apparent wind will come more from the true-wind direction. The change in apparent wind direction from the bottom of the mast to the top can be as much as 7 or 8 degrees. Sailmakers take this into account when building sails, by allowing more fullness at the top. This permits setting of the sail for the proper angle of attack at the top as well as the bottom. It is more popularly known as leech twist or, simply, twist. In light air, the velocity aloft will be proportionately stronger than at the deck level. Accordingly, more twist is needed in light winds than in strong. Twist is controlled by the sheet—less tension results in more twist. By using pinching strings, the bottom of the sail can be brought in, without the mainsheet tension that would eliminate the twist. Since there is little difference in the velocities at top and bottom in heavy air, less twist is needed, so heavy tension on the mainsheet eliminates much of the twist.

2

Sail Trim

THE PROBLEMS WHICH PLAGUE THE BEGINNER AND THE EXPERT ALIKE ARE:
How close into the wind should I sail when going to windward?
Where should I trim my sails? Where should my jib fairlead be?
Don't let the experts kid you; they don't always do it right either,
and two equally good skippers may have very different theories.
To further confuse the problem, a good skipper may have different
ideas at the end of each year; and for every theory why some things
should work, there are equally good ones why they shouldn't work.

Trim, as used in this context, is the adjustment of sails relative
to the centerline of the boat—that is, how the sail is aimed at the
wind—and is technically known as the angle of attack. Adjusting
the angle of attack of the mainsail is done with a traveler (and
related pinching strings) plus the mainsheet. All this can be done
without altering the draft and can be compared to swinging open
a barn door. By adjusting the traveler, the sail's inboard or outboard position can be changed, with no variation in the amount of
draft. When sailing off the wind, with the boom no longer over the
traveler, a switch occurs. The boom vang replaces the mainsheet
as the control for leech tension, and the mainsheet takes over the
function of the traveler in determining how far out the sail goes.

Generally for windward work, the boom should be trimmed so
that the end of the boom is about halfway between the centerline
of the boat and the gunwale. This position will, of course, vary
greatly with different types of boats, but the halfway position is a
good place to start. In very light winds, the boom should be brought
in closer to the centerline using the pinching strings, and tension

should be eased on the mainsheet. This prevents hooking of the leech and permits proper set of the twist. As the wind increases to a point where hiking is necessary, the pinching strings are released. As the wind continues to increase, the traveler is adjusted to pull the boom down more and in less. When the boat can no longer be held flat by hiking, the mainsheet must be eased. Keep the boom vang on tight to minimize the luffing of the top of the main. This easing of the main will reduce your heeling but cut down your driving force, so it should be used only as a last resort.

Similiar procedures are used with the jib. Athwartship adjustment is done by the Barber hauler, outboard tracks, or whatever equipment you use, but as noted before, it is more difficult, since the jib sheet controls tension as well. As with the mainsail, the jib should be trimmed loosely enough to eliminate leech hooking, and to insure proper set of the twist. As the wind increases, the jib sheet should be pulled in to the point that it is quite tight when you are in the fully hiked-out position. (When the conditions are such that the traveler has been eased, the jib fairlead should be moved outboard, both of which should be done in steps, as required to hold the boat flat.) If the boat is still heeling, and not going well, the fairlead should be moved aft. This relieves tension on the leech, and the top of the sail will luff.

In a high wind it is generally physically impossible to trim the jib too flat; however, when the wind is variable, and it usually is, it will be necessary to slack off the jib as the wind drops and pull it in again as the wind increases. The amount that the sheet is slacked off or trimmed in may be as little as ¼ inch, but that ¼ inch can make a real difference in the performance of the boat.

The fore-and-aft location of the jib fairlead should be determined by heading the boat into the wind slowly until the luff of the jib starts to luff. This luffing should take place simultaneously throughout the entire length of the jib luff. With the fairlead too far back, the luffing will start at the top; with the fairlead too far forward, it will start at the bottom. Many sailmakers are putting trim lines on jibs. This is a pencil line bisecting the clew and an extension of this line should point to the approximate fairlead location.

In order to understand the problems involved in trimming the mainsail, it will be a good idea to study Figure 2. The force acting on any airfoil may be considered as the resultant of the component of lift perpendicular to the chord line of the airfoil and of drag parallel to the chord line. (The chord line of an airfoil is a line going in the same general direction as the airfoil and is the line from which the airfoil is laid out. In the case of a sail, the chord

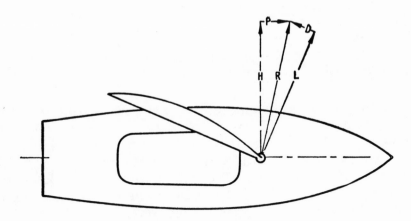

This diagram shows the forces acting on a sail with the wind in the direction shown.

    L is the lift force on the sail, perpendicular to the chord line.

    D is the drag or resistance acting parallel to the chord line.

    R is the resultant of L and D.

    P is the component of R parallel to the boat centerline, which makes the boat go.

    H is the component of R perpendicular to the boat centerline, which makes the boat heel and also drift.

FIGURE 2

line may be defined as a straight line connecting the luff and leech of the sail.) The resultant of these two forces may then be broken into a component parallel to the boat centerline, tending to make it go forward, and perpendicular to the boat centerline, tending to make it heel.

In the diagram, L is the lift component perpendicular to the chord line of the sail; D is the drag component parallel to the chord line; R is the resultant of D and L; P (for push) is the component of R parallel to the centerline of the boat; and H (for heel) is the component of R perpendicular to the centerline of the boat.

The component H is resisted by the combined resistance to lateral motion produced by the centerboard or keel, the rudder, and that part of the hull which is under water. Most of this lateral force is of course supplied by the centerboard or keel. Since these surfaces are symmetrical, they must move through the water at a slight angle to provide the necessary force. This means that the boat will drift slightly to leeward at any time that the wind is not from directly astern. The amount of this leeward drift depends on the amount of surface on the centerboard or keel, rudder, and hull, and also on the shape of the hull. With most well-designed small racing sailboats the angle of drift is so small that it is seldom noticed. Normal inaccuracies in steering on a reach, and wind shifts on a beat affect the course more than drift.

From the diagram, Figure 2, it may be seen that trimming the sail closer to the centerline of the boat permits the boat to head closer to the wind, but the force P becomes very small and eventually goes in reverse. By heading the boat farther out of the wind (assuming in all cases that the sail is trimmed to the point that it is just not quite luffing) the force P increases rapidly and the boat goes faster, but doesn't head as close into the wind.

Pointing a boat too closely into the wind is called pinching. The problem is: When are you pinching, and when aren't you? If a boat is pointed closer into the wind, it is on a better course and sails closer to the mark but makes less speed, as shown in the diagram. If it is pointed farther out of the wind it makes more speed, but the course is not as good. The problem arises in striking a happy medium. Pinching can be carried to such a degree that even the course achieved is not a good one, as the boat will lose enough speed so that it will slide sideways.

The effects of pinching or bearing off from the optimum heading are masked somewhat by the fact that the wind pennant shows the apparent wind direction, and this direction does not change as fast as the heading of the boat does. The apparent wind is the resultant of the actual wind direction and velocity and of the direction and velocity of the movement of the boat. If the boat is standing still, as it would be heading directly into a tide or river current whose speed was equal to the speed of the boat, the apparent wind and the actual wind would be from the same direction. As the speed of the boat increases, the difference between the direction and velocity of the apparent wind and the direction and velocity of the actual wind becomes greater. The sails are interested only in the apparent wind—they neither know nor care about the difference between apparent and actual wind. The skipper doesn't really need to bother about this difference either, as the actual wind is of academic interest only, but a knowledge of the relationship between the apparent and actual wind will help explain some situations that are confusing otherwise.

Different types of boats vary greatly in their ability to sail close to the wind. Large boats will generally sail closer to the wind than small ones; boats with a narrow beam will sail closer than those with a wide beam; and boats with tall masts and high aspect ratio sails will sail closer than those with shorter masts or gaff rigs. A representative number, which can be used for good small racing boats, is about 45 degrees out of the true wind.

Boats built to the same lines and having the same sails will all beat to windward best when the apparent wind is at the same angle to the centerline of the boat. However, a faster boat will be farther off the actual wind than a slow one will when sailing at the same angle to the apparent wind. The illustration, Figure 3, is exaggerated somewhat, but it shows that with a fast boat you should not try to point as high as the slower ones, and with a slow boat you will go best to windward pointing a little higher than the faster boats.

The numerical values given in the diagram, Figure 4, are not intended to apply exactly to any boat and are merely illustrative of what happens when a boat pinches or bears off from the best sailing angle when on a beat.

It will be seen that while the angle to the apparent wind changes only about half as much as the angle to the true wind, the speed of the boat, especially when pinching, changes rapidly. This is like compound interest as each decrease in boat speed decreases the apparent wind velocity which further decreases boat speed. This is why it is hard to learn just when you are pinching and when you are not.

In light winds many skippers make the mistake of trimming the main in too far without using pinching strings. When this is done, the leech is hooked and the twist is not set properly. It is very easy to put too much tension on the mainsheet, and you have to

TRUE AND APPARENT WINDS

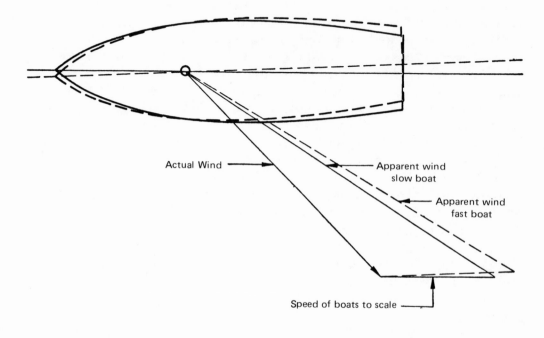

Actual Wind

Apparent wind
slow boat

Apparent wind
fast boat

Speed of boats to scale

The faster boat must sail farther off the true wind in order
to keep the apparent wind at the correct angle to the sails.

FIGURE 3

BOAT SAILING WITH WIND AT CORRECT ANGLE
FOR MOST EFFICIENT PROGRESS TO WINDWARD

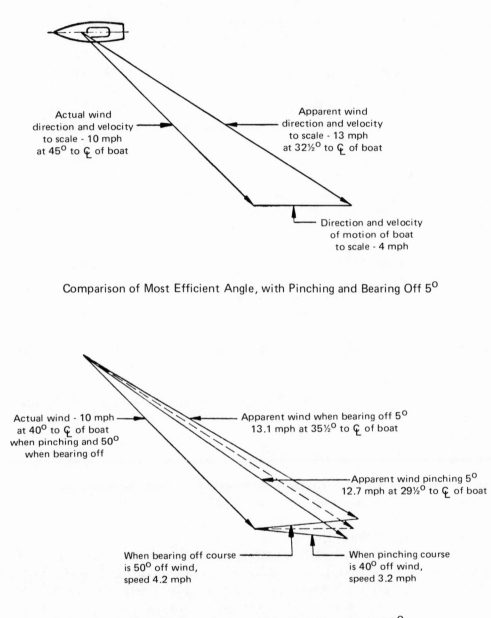

Actual wind direction and velocity to scale - 10 mph at 45° to ₵ of boat

Apparent wind direction and velocity to scale - 13 mph at 32½° to ₵ of boat

Direction and velocity of motion of boat to scale - 4 mph

Comparison of Most Efficient Angle, with Pinching and Bearing Off 5°

Actual wind - 10 mph at 40° to ₵ of boat when pinching and 50° when bearing off

Apparent wind when bearing off 5° 13.1 mph at 35½° to ₵ of boat

Apparent wind pinching 5° 12.7 mph at 29½° to ₵ of boat

When bearing off course is 50° off wind, speed 4.2 mph

When pinching course is 40° off wind, speed 3.2 mph

Although the angle to the actual wind has been changed 5°, the apparent wind changes only 3°

FIGURE 4

watch yourself constantly to keep from doing it. Both mainsheet and jib-sheet adjustments need to be watched continually in variable winds. If you cleat the main, you will have to adjust it frequently. If you don't cleat it, keep checking on yourself all the time —particularly if there are other boats close by. There is an almost irresistible tendency to start trimming the sheets too tightly when pressed by other boats.

Remember that the ability of a boat to point high is determined by the angle of attack of the sails. In light to medium winds and flat water, much can be gained by going high. Sails should be trimmed in as much as possible but still keeping proper draft. Do not overdo this, since to gain pointing ability, you have to sacrifice speed. Achieving the happy medium is difficult. When encountering heavy wind and big waves, the most important thing is to keep the boat moving. Speed is essential to keep the boat going through the waves. If you are too close to the wind your speed is reduced and you are more likely to be stopped dead by a big wave.

The combination of a light to medium wind and a heavy chop is an extremely difficult one to handle, and takes a great deal of practice to master. Bearing off in this manner so as not to point so high in waves will seem to conflict with advice to be given later on the handling of a boat in high winds and big waves. This is another one of those cases where it is necessary to decide which of several factors is the most important in making the boat go fast, then doing the important thing and ignoring the unimportant— regardless of theory.

The technique of high-wind sailing will be covered separately later, but the change in technique with increasing wind and waves may be summarized as follows: in a light wind and no waves, point up into the wind until you are on the verge of luffing. With increasing waves, bear off a bit farther. Sail at this point until the wind b⸍ comes so high that in spite of getting out of the boat as far as possible, it heels too much. Then head into the wind enough so you can balance the boat until you approach the point of luffing. After that, slack off the main.

In connection with this problem of deciding how close into the wind you should sail, it will probably seem to you that every boat on the water is pointing higher than yours. Generally this is purely psychological; occasionally it may be due to the fact that the boat you happen to be watching has just gotten a nice puff, and it is generally better just to forget about it. However, if boats some distance off from you are definitely pointing higher all the time, this may mean that the wind is better over there and you had better go over and investigate; but *do not under any circum-*

stances attempt to point as high as you think the others are merely by heading your boat closer into the wind and pinching.

An experienced skipper can tell fairly well by the feel of his boat whether or not he is pointing it too high, except when the wind is practically nonexistent, but it is a good idea even for an experienced skipper to occasionally head the boat a little more into the wind and watch the jib and then bear off a little bit and just make sure that he was right. This feel is difficult to describe, as it is made up of many things, not all of them tangible. In medium and light winds, the angle of heel will lessen just as you start pointing too high; in a medium-to-high wind where the waves are not too high, the slapping of the waves against the hull will slow down as you point too high; in a very high wind there will generally be fairly big waves which will stop you noticeably if you are too high. In a very light wind where the wind won't even cause a piece of yarn to move, much less the sail, all that anyone can do is light a cigarette and steer by the smoke. Many skippers say they can sense the speed of the boat by the feel of the tiller. I have never been able to do this, as I never could detect any difference in the feel of the tiller until it was too late and I was already headed too high.

One inexpensive piece of equipment that many skippers have is a wind direction indicator or tell tale. This is a piece of material such as yarn, plastic, or light spinnaker cloth attached to the sail. I prefer yarn as it is less likely to stick to the sail. If the air flow is not parallel to the sail, eddies will occur and the yarn shows this right away. The yarn should be about 6 inches long and taped to both sides of the jib, 6 to 8 inches back from the luff. Put one a third of the way up the luff from the deck and another two-thirds of the way up, and on both sides of the sail. When sailing too high the tell tale on the windward side will flutter and point up, even before the luff breaks. Sailing too low will cause the tell tale on the leeward side to flutter and gyrate. When the leeward tell tale is steady, pointing aft, and the windward one floats easily aft and slightly upward, the jib is at its proper angle of attack. Some skippers use tell tales on the mainsail, but this is not as successful because of the interference of the mast.

The most important thing to remember about going to windward is: you can't go along mentally picking daisies and beat the other boats to the windward mark. You must constantly be on the alert. This advice sounds trite, but it is amazing how many skippers could improve their scores by taking it to heart. Another good thing to remember is that most skippers point too high. It is difficult to tell just where the perfect point is, and it is a lot better to be a *little* too far off the wind than to be too close to it. Getting to the windward mark first is what counts—not trying to see who can outpoint whom.

On a reach the same principles apply concerning the trimming of sails—that is, let them out as far as possible without luffing. Most skippers trim their sails too flat on a reach. Generally it is not desirable to cleat the sheets when on a reach. The sails should be pulled in and the boat headed upwind as the wind drops; the sheets should be slacked off, and the boat should be headed out of the wind in gusts. In a medium light wind it is probably better just to hold a straight course, but to adjust the sheets for proper trim with variations of wind velocity. In very light winds it may pay to follow very much of a zigzag course, bearing off fairly far with puffs in order to ride them as long as possible, then heading up quite far after the puff has passed in order to get the next one sooner. This doesn't always work, but it is worth a try.

Except in a light wind, the boom vang should always be rigged when on a reach or a run. It should be pulled quite tight so that the leech of the sail falls off as little as possible near the top. Rig it even in a light wind, if there are waves left over from a wind now gone or from power boats tearing around. (I know now why the cattlemen used to shoot the sheepherders and vice versa. It's a good thing that culture got to the West before sailboats did. The advent of water skiing makes one long for the good old days.)

There is much difference of opinion as to the point at which the jib should be poled out on the side opposite the main when on a broad reach. It is my opinion that this should be done as soon as the wind pennant points in a direction straight across the beam of the boat, except in very high winds where the pole will be hard to get out, or if it may be necessary to head upwind at any time in the near future. Setting the whisker pole at this point requires a long pole or the jib will not fill properly. I carry two whisker poles on my Snipe, one 90 inches long and one 86 inches—the longer one being preferred for broad reaching and the shorter one for a run. Either one can be used in either case if you happen to lose a pole in a high wind, which frequently happens. Most boats do not have whisker poles long enough to get the best efficiency out of the jib when set with the wind directly abeam. With a short pole, they have to let the pole go well forward before the jib will draw, giving a very inefficient shape to the jib.

Even with a long pole, it is not advisable to wing out when the apparent wind is much forward of directly across the boat. From this point forward it is better to take in the pole immediately. In trimming the jib with the pole out, just the opposite to the usual rule should be followed; the jib should be pulled back as far as possible instead of letting the sheet out as far as possible.

The apparent wind direction at which the spinnaker may be hoisted on a reach is about the same as the point at which the jib should be poled out. The spinnaker can be carried in a very light wind with the apparent wind about a half point ahead of the beam, but as the wind velocity increases this point moves back until when the wind is at about the maximum at which you can handle the spinnaker, the apparent wind should be about a point behind the beam.

In putting either the whisker pole or spinnaker pole out, the crew should not go any farther forward than is absolutely necessary. In a light wind, his moving around will shake the sails, and in a high wind the boat is likely to broach if the crew gets very far forward on the deck. It is generally best for the skipper to handle the sheet until the crew has the pole set unless there are more than two people on the boat; and in very high winds when difficulty will be experienced in getting the pole out, the boat should be headed directly downwind, the pole should be pushed out straight ahead, and then the sail pulled back with the sheet after the pole has been set on the mast. Do not try to hold the sail back by bending the pole —all you will accomplish is breaking the pole. Just push on the pole, and trim with the sheet.

On a reach the jib fairlead should be farther out from the centerline of the boat than on a beat. If your fairleads are well in from the sheer, you can use a snatch block on the sheer if you do not have a Barber hauler. In light winds the skipper or one of the crew can hold the sheet anywhere desired, but a pole cannot be used under the racing rules.

When reaching with a spinnaker, the sheet should be led as far aft and as far out as possible. The spinnaker pole should be trimmed so that it is at an angle of from 90 to 110 degrees to the apparent wind, depending on the boat, the length of the pole, and the cut of the spinnaker.

A good wind indicator is essential in order to tell when to set the spinnaker or whisker pole and to be able to tell on a run when you are about to jibe. About the most reliable, and certainly the cheapest, wind indicator is a piece of yarn tied to each shroud. Yarn on the shrouds is not accurate on a run because of the flow of air around the mast off the main, but this can easily be allowed for. The yarn will indicate a jibe coming on before you are actually ready for a jibe. Generally, the yarn will make an angle of about 10 degrees to the centerline of the boat when the wind is dead astern. If you have a backstay, use a piece of yarn on it. It is not as accurate as a mast fly but is an improvement over yarn located on the shrouds. Some skippers try to use the mast fly or shroud yarns on a beat to tell whether they are pointing properly.

I don't think this is at all efficient, at least on small boats, as the difference between pinching and not pinching is only a degree or so, and no wind indicator can give that accurate an indication. I look at the yarn on the stays frequently on a beat, particularly in a light shifty wind, just to be sure that I haven't been absent-minded and headed way off below where I should be pointing, but that is the only use I make of it on a beat.

In a light wind which may turn into a drifting match, be sure to have a supply of fireworks, lighting punk or lots of cigarettes and a lighter on board, as any kind of a wind indicator is worthless when little zephyrs of wind are coming from all directions when and if they come at all, and frequently these little zephyrs won't have any visible effect on the sails. Under these circumstances, there is nothing to sail by except the smoke.

The punk, which is recommended for nonsmokers, is available in the United States around July 4th anywhere in the country, and at any time of year in the South. It burns very slowly and makes a lot of smoke. You will probably be accused of burning incense but if it distracts the competitors, so much the better.

To summarize and give a general rule, several conditions are listed below, together with what you should do with your sails. Bear in mind there are exceptions, but these rules should serve for the vast majority of time. Make a habit of looking at your sails to see if they have proper draft and trim. Learn to use the various controls so that if an adjustment is needed, it becomes automatic.

DRIFTERS—Put a lot of draft and twist in the sails, and since you are not trying to point high, trim the sheets very loosely.

LIGHT TO MEDIUM WINDS AND FLAT WATER—This is a pointing situation, so remove draft from the sails and trim firmly. Don't strap in so hard that the sails become distorted and all the twist is removed.

LIGHT TO MEDIUM WINDS WITH WAVES OR CHOP—This is a footing condition so don't point high. More draft is needed than for flat water. Trim ever so slightly less than for flat water.

HEAVY WINDS AND WAVES—Generally these two go together but there is probably more wind than you need, so remove as much draft as possible, using a lot of tension on the sheets. Put the traveler and jib fairleads outboard and don't pinch. Keep the boat moving and flat, luffing through the gusts.

SURVIVAL CONDITIONS—Do more of everything called for in Heavy

Winds and Waves. Hang on and pray. And remember that the more experience you get, the fewer times you will encounter survival conditions. Life-preserver vests don't do any good stowed away in the boat—wear them. You will be surprised how many experienced sailors do even when not forced to.

3

Handling the Boat

THE MOST IMPORTANT THING ABOUT HANDLING THE BOAT IS TO HOLD IT as flat as possible. This of course does not apply to the inland-lake scow, or similar boats which are designed to sail on their ear, but with any other type of small boat you won't go anywhere if you let the boat heel.

It may be lots of fun to sail around with your lee rail under, but your smarter racing competitors will be very happy to see you do so. The boat should not be allowed to heel more than 10 or 15 degrees even momentarily. In drifting conditions it is helpful to force the boat to heel 20 or so degrees by sitting on the low side. This will enable gravity to help what little wind there is to fill the sails properly and at the same time reduce the wetted surface. At all other times hold the boat as flat as possible.

The chief means of holding a small sailboat flat is for the skipper and crew to get out as far as possible in order to balance the boat. This does not mean just sitting on the edge of the boat. The skipper and the crew should be provided with straps or some other device to hook their feet under in order to enable them to really get out. This, of course, is a little hard on the stomach muscles, but it is really astonishing how much faster a boat will move when the skipper and crew lean out so that their legs are straight, their bodies are horizontal, and they are entirely outside of the boat except from their feet up to their knees. The length of the extension on the tiller should be such that the skipper can get out this way and allow the tiller to remain near the center of the boat, which is where it will be if the boat is rigged properly and it is not allowed to heel.

Many skippers and crews used to think that by merely draping themselves along or over the sheer, they were doing a high-class job of balancing the boat. Maybe it was a result of a mistaken desire to reduce air resistance—but in any case, it was mistaken. The important thing in a high wind is to hold the boat flat—the increased drive of the boat will more than compensate for the air resistance of the upper halves of a couple of bodies projecting horizontally from the sheer. The center of gravity of the human form moves about 16½ inches farther out when horizontal, and perpendicular to the boat centerline, than when draped along the sheer. So get your body out as far as possible. If you are young and agile, arrange your hiking straps so you get all your body above the knees outside the boat. Since it is physically impossible to hold your body horizontal for too long, you end up sitting on the side of the boat. When a gust comes in and you need more leverage, you straighten out your body to a horizontal position.

A rather spectacular and very effective way of balancing the boat is for the crew to stand on the sheer leaning out from this point by hanging onto a line tied either to the mast or to the shrouds. This method can be used only with fairly steady winds and requires a young and agile crew. Also, the lines he uses to hang onto occasionally get tangled in the jib sheet, but if the crew has had enough practice at it and is very sure-footed, it is a very effective means of holding the boat down when this cannot be done by merely hiking out of the boat.

You will recognize this method as the basis for the trapeze rigs on such boats as a Flying Dutchman and a 505. It has been developed to a very sophisticated point involving special body harness and support wires. This enables the crew to stand on the sheer in a horizontal position—getting his entire body outside the boat. The amount of leverage can be varied by the crew flexing his knees to a crouching position. It is the ultimate of effectiveness in holding the boat flat. In fact, it has made possible the performance of these boats—they just could not be sailed in heavy winds using the normal hiking positions.

In the sketch, Figure 5, an equation is set up for the lateral and vertical forces acting on a 450-pound sailboat when it is heeling at a 15-degree angle to illustrate the value of really getting out to balance a small boat. Five different positions are shown for the center-of-gravity locations of skippers and crews balancing the boat by various means. The respective locations, the moment arms, and the amount of heeling tendency that can be balanced by

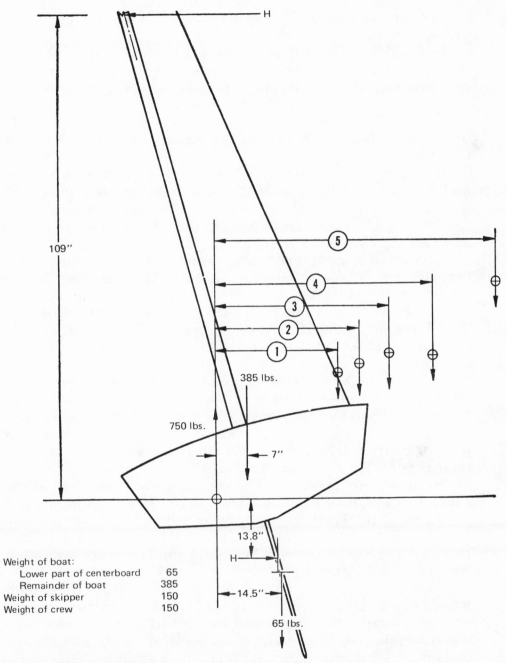

H = Force tending to heel boat
    (resisted by equal force at center of lateral resistance)
X = Moment arm to center of gravity of skipper
Y = Moment arm to center of gravity of crew

Basic equation for equilibrium: Σ Mo: $H = \dfrac{150X + 150Y + (385 \times 7) + (65 \times 14.5)}{(109 + 13.8)}$

$H = 1.22X + 1.22Y + 30$

FIGURE 5

a 150-pound skipper and a 150-pound crew (5 feet, 10 inches tall) are as follows:

In Position 1, the skipper and crew are leaning out, but with their feet braced against the opposite side of the cockpit. Their moment arm is 28 inches and the value of H is therefore:

$$28(1.22) + 28(1.22) + 30 = 98.5 \text{ lbs.}$$

The moment arm of a skipper and crew lying on their stomachs with their feet hanging over the sheer is the same as Position 1.

In Position 2, the skipper and crew are draped along the sheer and are well streamlined—if they can hold the boat down with their moment arm which is 33 inches, which will balance a heeling force of 110.8 pounds, 13 percent more than with the skipper and crew in Position 1.

In Position 3, the skipper and crew are doing what most people consider a good job of balancing a boat—but their legs are not straight, and their bodies are at about a 45-degree angle instead of horizontal. Their moment arm is 40.5 inches, and the heeling force they can balance is 129 pounds, 31 percent more than with the skipper and crew in Position 1, and 16 percent more than in Position 2.

In Position 4, both the skipper and crew are doing an excellent job of getting out—their legs are straight and their bodies are horizontal. Their moment arm is 49.5 inches, and the heeling force which they can balance is 151 pounds, almost 54 percent more than in Position 1, and 17 percent more than in Position 3 which most people think is pretty good.

Position 5 is the center of gravity of a crew standing on the sheer, hanging onto a line attached to the stay, leaning out at a 45-degree angle. The heeling tendency which can be balanced by the crew in this position, with the skipper in Position 4, is 168.5 pounds, 72 percent more than Position 1 and 12 percent better than with both at Position 4.

Figure 6 shows Dave Chapin and his crew doing an excellent job of holding down a Snipe on a beat. It also illustrates proper use of hiking straps. At the moment the picture was snapped, Dave was not hiking out as far as he could because the wind had apparently dropped momentarily; however, they are completely out of the boat except for their legs from slightly above the knees, and when a gust comes Dave could immediately hike out farther and keep the boat from heeling any more. The angle of heel to which they are holding the boat is about as close to vertical as is practical.

To illustrate the relative importance of the skipper and crew as compared with the centerboard in balancing the boat, a 150-

(Sam Chapin)

FIGURE 6
DAVE CHAPIN SHOWS HOW TO HIKE OUT.

pound skipper and crew moving their center of gravity one-half inch farther out on a Snipe is equivalent to increasing the weight of the centerboard from 62 to 80 pounds when the boat is held to a 15-degree angle of heel. The flatter the boat is held, the less the centerboard counts.

Holding the boat flat is just as important on a reach as on a beat, especially when there is enough wind for the boat to plane. Some boats even go better heeled to windward on a reach in a medium wind. The fore-and-aft balance of the boat should be slightly forward of that on a beat, particularly in very light winds.

With heavier and larger boats, the crew weight becomes a smaller percentage of the total and the effect on balance of the skipper and crew getting out becomes less. The effect will still be appreciable, however, until you get to a fairly large boat, and even here, it may be just enough to make the difference between winning and not winning in a close race.

There is no such thing as an absolutely steady wind, as far as either direction or velocity is concerned. This means that if the boat is being balanced for the average wind, it will tend to heel over in the gusts. If the wind is not too high, the boat can be balanced by the skipper and crew getting out farther in the gust and crawling back as the gust passes. If they are already out as far as they can go balancing the wind before the gust, something else must be done. On a reach, slack off the main and bear off in the gust. Head back up and pull in the main when the gust passes.

When beating to windward and the skipper and crew are out as far as they can get balancing the average wind, the thing to do in the gust is to head the boat into the wind slightly, letting the jib luff until the gust is past. It takes a lot of practice to head the boat into the wind soon enough to prevent any additional heeling over and then to head it back out of the wind again at the right moment to prevent the boat heeling to windward, but the boat can be kept at a constant angle of heel through a gust without the crew moving.

With the slide and car type of traveler, an expert skipper or crew can ease the traveler instead of luffing through puffs. It takes an easily adjusted traveler rigged in the center to do this. It also requires a bit of strength to bring the traveler back to its normal position. It would appear to me that luffing through the puffs is faster with the advantage of gaining some distance to windward.

If the waves are not too high, the gust may be seen coming on the surface of the water; however, with high waves the gust must be felt and the tiller pushed down immediately. It is for this reason that it is necessary to have a good tiller extension, as the boat must sometimes be luffed very sharply to prevent heeling.

Luffing through gusts is an astonishingly effective way of keeping the boat going and working to windward at the same time. I have watched two boats sailing close together running into the same gust; the boat which luffs into the puff will gain about 10 feet in forward distance and about 3 or 4 feet in progress to windward over the other boat which is merely allowed to heel with the gust. If the other skipper slacks off his main also to stop the heeling, the boat which has luffed into the gust will gain as much as 20 feet.

I have worked out of a hopeless position immediately behind another boat and worked past him to windward or to leeward on about three gusts when the other boat was allowed to heel. I have also been taken by another boat on a couple of gusts when I wasn't sharp enough to luff immediately and the other skipper was. This advice may seem to be contrary to the earlier advice to not point quite as high in high waves, as high winds are normally accompanied by waves; however, the luffing recommended here is only in gusts and the boat should be immediately headed off the wind to its best sailing point as soon as it is possible for the skipper and crew to hold the boat flat.

It took only about one minute to read the preceding paragraphs, but it will take a year or two to be able to work out the technique that I am talking about. It took me eight years, but nobody told me what to do in words of one syllable that sank in— I finally figured it out by watching John Hayward beat me every time the wind blew hard. John had written an article a year or so before on the subject of reducing weather helm by luffing, but it didn't sink in.

I also have a suspicion that many skippers will say that maybe it works on a Snipe but it won't work on their boats. This is another case where Mr. Kettering was right—they know it won't work because that just isn't the way to sail in high winds. I have done it in a Hagerty Sea Shell, and I have seen it done—very rarely, but successfully—on Sea Gulls, and a friend of mine who sails on the Pacific tells me it works on his 46-foot yawl, so the technique is not limited to small boats. Unfortunately, the majority of my competitors now seem to have adopted the system.

Maybe the reason it took me so long is that in Kansas the gusts come quicker, blow harder, and quit more suddenly than any place else that I have ever sailed. The wind also has a nasty habit of shifting very suddenly about 15 degrees every now and then when it is blowing hard, with the result that in Wichita you are more apt to capsize to windward than to leeward in a high wind, and a skipper has a pardonable tendency to pay more attention to staying right side up than he does to learning the finer points of luffing through gusts. Any place else, the technique should be a lot easier to perfect.

A good way to practice is to go out when the wind is not too high and practice holding the boat to a constant angle of heel by using the tiller without the skipper or crew moving. Another good way to practice this, without involving too much effort, is to go in a high wind without the jib and try the same thing. Leaving off the jib will let you practice longer before you are worn out.

If you are going to win races in high winds, this technique must be developed. You have to learn to practically smell the gust coming and start to luff before it gets there and to start to bear off before it leaves. Keep your mainsheet cleated all the time. *Do not,* except as a last resort, let out your main.

Sailing with the main cleated in a high wind is a big help to the skipper when coming about, as he pays no attention to the mainsheet and concentrates on balancing the boat and getting it headed on its new course. Leaving the main cleated in a high wind will scare the skipper badly at first, but when he has developed the technique of luffing into the gusts he will be astonished at how seldom it is necessary to ever uncleat the main on a beat. Probably the biggest advantage, however, is that keeping the main cleated in a high wind will *force* the skipper to learn to luff through the puffs and therefore to sail his boat most efficiently.

The cleat should, of course, be arranged so that it can be released immediately, and the skipper should always hold the sheet in case it should be necessary to release it when sailing in high winds. After a considerable amount of practice, it is possible to sail in winds up to 35 miles an hour without ever uncleating the main on a beat even in the gusty winds experienced in the Midwest. In addition to not having to bother about the mainsheet when coming about, cleating of the main allows the skipper to devote his attention to handling the boat, watching others, and in a high wind allows him to save his energy for balancing the boat instead of fighting the mainsheet.

On most small boats the fore-and-aft location of the skipper and the crew should be approximately in the center of the boat, sitting a little farther forward in light winds with no waves and farther back with higher winds and high waves. The weight should generally be carried farther forward on a reach and a run than on a beat—except, when approaching planing conditions, it will be necessary to be quite far back. Each boat is somewhat different, and it takes experimentation to find the correct locations. I quickly learned how far back you need to be when hit by a particularly heavy gust on a broad reach and the boat nosed into a wave and headed for the bottom. I was certainly thankful that the boat had a forward deck and spray rails.

In light winds the most important thing is to sit still and not jump around in the boat. When it is necessary to move, move slowly so as not to shake out what little wind there is in the sails. When it is not necessary to get out to balance the boat, the crew should sit in the bottom of the boat. It may seem silly to worry about such a small thing as air resistance on the skipper and crew in a light wind; however, many times the difference between first and second place in a race will be one second in a race lasting several hours. In this case the person losing the race would have only had to improve his speed by a factor of 1.0001 in order to win. This may also sound contradictory to my remarks made earlier about trying to save wind resistance in a high wind by draping yourself over the sheer. It isn't—it is merely a question of deciding which is most important under the existing conditions. In a high wind, it is most important to balance the boat. In lighter winds this can be done easily, so it is most important to cut down wind resistance.

In light winds the sails should generally be handled slowly when the course of the boat is changed. One exception is when jibing. In this case the main should be pulled in fast, then let out slowly on the opposite side. Hauling in the boom with the sheets is too slow—the boom should be pulled in by the crew handling the boom itself, not the sheets.

Very high waves, especially those which are close together and therefore steep, create a special set of problems for a small boat. The most important thing under these conditions is to keep the boat dry. Generally the largest waves will come in groups. There will be several waves which are larger than the average, but these large waves do not generally extend over very much distance. When beating to windward, keep an eye out for these groups of larger waves and avoid them if possible. This may be done by luffing up to let them go past or bearing off and getting by them before they get to you. When you cannot miss them, the proper technique is to bear off just a little just before the top of the wave. If the next wave is not too close you can head up again, even to the point of luffing slightly, as you coast down the wave—then bear off just before the top of the next wave. If the waves are too close together to do this, as they will be in shallow water, you can at least do it on every other wave. Just go ahead and crash through the intervening ones. When the waves are breaking, bearing off is dangerous as the boat may be filled with water by a single wave, or it may just simply be knocked over by the force of the wave. In this case, it is better to luff up and head as nearly as possible into the wave. You will still take on plenty of water, but there is less chance of being swamped or capsized.

In a high wind (35 miles an hour or so) on a very close reach, it will sometimes be necessary to slack off the main slightly in order to cut down the forward drive of the sails tending to nose the bow under, even though you can balance the boat with the sails trimmed in. It is possible under these conditions with the sails trimmed for the best speed to drive the boat so hard that the bow will not rise over the crest of the waves, and a great deal of water will be taken on even though the waves are not too high. In these circumstances it is better to slack off the main a little bit until the bow rides over the waves better. Moving the skipper and the crew quite far aft helps, but is not completely effective, as the drive of the sails is so much greater than the effect of movement of the skipper-and-crew weight. This happens on rare occasions, but it does happen.

Always remember, in bad waves it is important to keep as much water out of the boat as possible; a boat with very much water in it just simply will not go. The reason is the weight—water weighs 62 pounds per cubic foot, and this weight is uncontrollable. It would be nice if it would help you hold the boat flat but it won't; it always goes to the low side. These are the times when you appreciate the double bottoms and self-bailing devices—99 percent of the time you can keep on sailing and pay no attention to the water taken in, as it will soon be gone. However, on occasion, a really big one climbs aboard your boat, and it is usually the one you didn't see coming. At this point it is essential to devote all of your attention to balancing the boat. When most of the water is gone you can resume your racing. If you didn't balance you can practice your "righting a capsized boat" technique.

When beating to windward in big waves, make up your mind about tacking as far ahead of time as possible. There will be patches where the waves are smaller just like there are patches where they are larger than average, and the boat should be brought about in these patches where possible. In any case, do not hit a wave just as the boat heads into the wind, as the boat is very likely to stop and go in irons. Going into irons in a high wind with big waves is a hazardous and very unprofitable occupation. Even if you want to tack for the mark, and will overstand the mark if you keep going, it is still better to do so—no matter how quickly you can right a capsized boat.

What to do when you get caught in a squall or thunderstorm depends of course on how bad the storm is going to be. The problem is to tell this before it is too late. In the Midwest, when you see a big black cloud and lightning, you can expect the worst. If the race committee is smart, they will call off the race before the storm gets too close. If they don't, as soon as the wind shifts and starts to come out of the storm, head into the wind, drop your sails, and get the anchor out. In the Midwest, discretion is definitely the better part of valor in a thunderstorm, as winds over 70 miles an hour are customary. I tried sailing through one going to windward on the jib after dropping the main once and broke a mast in the process. I tried sailing through another one because it came up in the course of a race in the Midwestern Snipe Championship. The weather bureau reported the wind at 75 miles an hour afterward. The boat I had at that time had a cockpit only 18 inches wide, and while strictly speaking we didn't capsize, our method of getting to shore was somewhat unorthodox. My crew was standing on the centerboard holding the jib sheet while I was in the water holding onto the rudder. The top of the mast would get 3 or 4 feet above the water before getting slapped down again, but we got to shore without any water in the boat. I don't recommend this procedure, however. The only reason it worked here was that the storm came up suddenly on a small lake and the waves did not have time to build up, and also we were not far from shore. Those hailstones bouncing off your head don't feel good.

Along the coast, the storms are not normally so severe and it is generally possible to sail through them. The safest place to be when a storm hits is heading into it on a beat. On a reach you are apt to be blown over even with all sails free if the wind is over 50 miles an hour; and on a run you may easily lose your mast, particularly if you don't have a permanent backstay. If the wind stays over about 45 miles an hour for any length of time, you will do better by dropping the jib. It is surprising how well a normally sloop-rigged boat will handle in a squall under the main alone, particularly if you have been fighting it with a good-sized genoa up.

If the wind has been blowing fairly hard up to the time the squall hits (which it generally doesn't in the case of a thunderstorm) a run may be the safest place to be caught by the storm, as the boat will be moving fast and the impact of the blow may then not be hard enough to dismast you. The chief disadvantage of a run is that it will be difficult, if not impossible, to head up to a beat without capsizing if you run out of water before the squall lets up, and it is likely to be difficult to drop your sails on a run without damage to your main.

In any case—if you see a storm coming, drop your boom as low as you can while you still have a chance, reef if you can, and put on your life preservers. And if you are really smart, you will consider safety first, and the possibility of winning the race, if there is still a race, secondary.

When coming about, the crew should always release the jib the instant that it starts to luff (do not hold it until it is backwinded), and in high winds the skipper and crew should get to the high side, hike all the way out, and trim the sails all at the same time. The crew should not attempt to cleat the jib sheet while crossing to the other side as too much time will be lost. The cleats should be arranged so that the sheet can be cleated and uncleated from the hiked-out position; the crew should cleat the sheet just as he is hiking out. As he hikes out he can use body leverage to put the necessary tension on the sheet. This whole procedure is not easy to accomplish in high winds, but it is of vital importance.

Some skippers recommend bearing off slightly to get the boat started after tacking. This is necessary if you have allowed the boat to stop by turning on either too small or too large a radius, but with a small boat it shouldn't be necessary. It is particularly bad in a high wind as it will be necessary to slack off on the sheets to keep from heeling too much when bearing off, and it will be difficult to get them trimmed in again. Remember—get over fast, get way out, and trim the jib in flat. The important thing is to hold the boat down flat and get it moving on its new tack immediately after it is in a position where the sails will fill. If you do all of this fast enough, you won't need to bear off to get the boat moving again.

If a stop is rigged to limit the rudder travel, the skipper can merely let go of the tiller when he wants to come about and pick it up when he gets to the opposite side. In a light wind, the tiller should be given a good shove before releasing it, and with no wind it may be necessary to pump it quite a bit to get the boat around. While sculling is of course illegal, assisting the boat to come about when there isn't any wind has been allowed providing the tiller is not moved beyond the centerline of the boat in the process.

In boats light enough so that the weight of the occupants can have a significant effect on the amount the boat heels, there is a technique known as roll-tacking which is very efficient in light to moderate winds. When you are ready to tack, heel the boat fairly rapidly through an angle of 30 or more degrees to windward, while you shove the tiller or just let it go to leeward. The roll swings the sails into the wind giving an increase in the apparent wind velocity and therefore a momentary increase in lift. Also, the sails stay filled and drawing longer before luffing. As the boat rounds on to the new tack, the skipper and crew cross to the other side, and since the boat is heeled to leeward (the old windward side), they now hike out sharply to bring the boat upright. This second hike does the same as the first and you have gained several feet over a boat that doesn't roll-tack. The technique requires crew coordination and practice to develop it into one continuous flowing motion. It is most effective in light winds but can be used in anything up to the point when you can't heel the boat to windward because of too much wind.

When jibing, never turn loose of the tiller as it will be on the wrong side of the cockpit when you have finished your jibe, and it may be hard to get hold of it soon enough. Also, your jibe is likely to be much too fast with the tiller free. In a high wind always uncleat the mainsheet and hold it in your hand while jibing. Nothing will capsize you faster than having the mainsheet get snarled up when jibing in a high wind.

Many skippers consider jibing in a high wind to be hazardous and prefer to come about even if it means overshooting a mark. While a jibe in a high wind is admittedly a pretty wild maneuver, I feel that in a small boat properly rigged there is less chance of capsizing in a well-done jibe in a very high wind than there is by being caught by a puff just as you are finished coming about and before you have regained your forward speed.

In high wind on a broad reach or run, most small boats will climb up out of the water and plane like a speed boat. Minimum weight and smooth underwater surfaces are particularly important in getting the boat to start planing as soon as possible. Keeping the boat flat is also essential. With small waves such as are found on inland lakes even with high winds, not very much can be done to make the boat plane when it is on the verge of it or to keep it planing when it wants to stop, except to be very careful of the trim of the sails when reaching; however, on big waves on either a run or a very broad reach, the boat will plane on the top of the waves like a surfboard. Planing can be promoted by "pumping," which is frequent rapid trimming of the sails. To be most effective, the sail should be trimmed in very fast, then eased out a little more slowly. The racing rules permit pumping ONLY to promote planing; pumping is prohibited after the boat has started to plane. "Ooching," which consists of lunging forward and stopping abruptly, is considered in the same category as pumping under the racing rules. When the boat starts to plane, the skipper and crew should move well aft, especially when there are waves present that the boat might try to dive under.

A planing jibe can be simple if properly planned and executed, or it can be a catastrophe. Catastrophe can strike early if an overeager crew goes to what is going to be the windward side but has not quite become that, if a puff happens to hit at the same time. The main has been trimmed in and the boat capsizes to leeward, putting the crew in the water before the skipper can turn loose of the main. More often catastrophe strikes after the jibe has been completed because the boat is not properly balanced and it broaches.

When running dead before the wind with no mark involved or if only a small course change is involved, follow the procedure shown in Figure 7. The centerboard should be all the way down and the procedure should be started, if possible, when the boat is going as fast as possible in relation to the wind. This can occur immediately after the boat has accelerated from a gust, when there is a momentary lull in the wind, or when you are surfing down a wave. By having the pole set before the jibe, the boat will be balanced after the jibe and no trouble should be experienced.

When making a large course change, the pole should be taken in, if it has been out, shortly before the boom is ready to go over, leaving the jib on the side opposite the boom, with the sheet cleated about where you will want it after the jibe. If you have been on a reach, head fairly far above the mark planning to bear off and trim the main so that you are dead before the wind when you get even with it. At that point, pull the jib over and cleat it before the boom comes over. The centerboard should be left where it was on the reach, which will probably be about halfway up. The board should be all the way down in a jibe at a mark only when jibing a downwind mark onto a beat.

When a jibe to a reach is completed with the jib set, the boat will pop right up on a plane if the skipper and crew are hiked out ready to go. If the jib is not trimmed or if a good hiking job is not done, the boat will take off to windward completely out of control and disaster is not far away.

With really high waves, all rules are off as far as where the skipper and crew should sit when reaching or running. Planing on waves will generally start better by having the weight fairly far forward. This is all right as long as the top of the stem is still above the water, but if the bow dives under, get back as far as possible, and quickly. This maneuver generally ends up with the skipper sitting on the transom with the tiller over his head and the crew on his lap. For some reason, wiggling the tiller rapidly back and forth seems to help unsubmerge. Another time when discretion is the better part of valor is when planing on the crest of waves which are close together and really high. In this case the entire front half of the boat will be out of the water hanging over the trough in front of the wave, and the skipper and crew had better

JIBING IN A HIGH WIND

Start to bear off, put out whisker pole on same side as main, and cleat the jib sheet so the pole won't fall down. Continue to bear off while pulling in on main. When the boom is almost ready to go over, crew should help it.

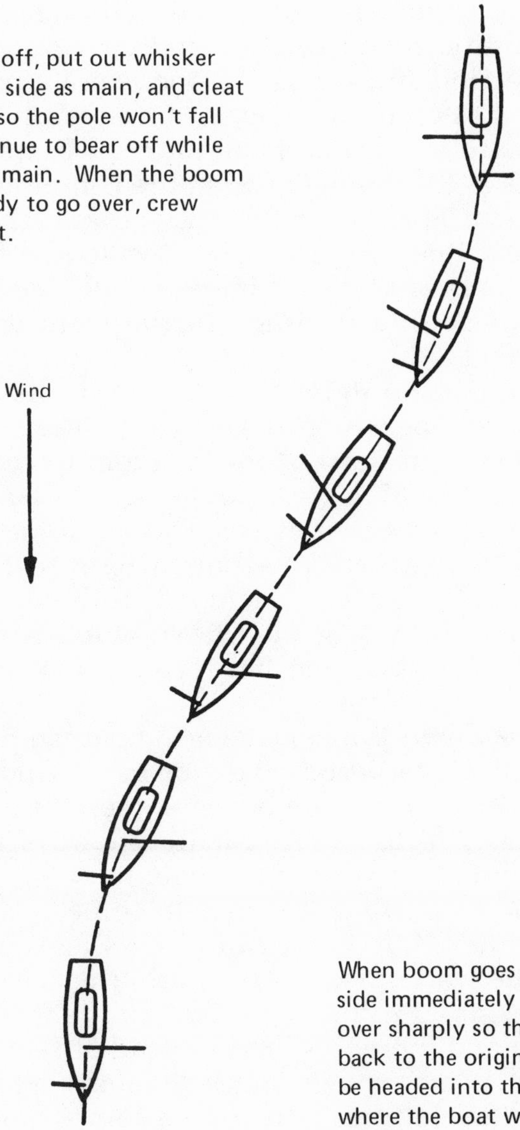

Wind

When boom goes over, get to the high side immediately and pull the tiller over sharply so that you will get back to the original course and not be headed into the wind, which is where the boat will try to go if you don't prevent it.

FIGURE 7

be sitting on the transom. Due to the fact that the water right at the crest of the wave is moving faster than the wave when the wave is on the verge of breaking, the boat will sometimes practically take off and fly when the wave on which it is planing decides to break. It scoots up onto the next wave ahead and starts planing there. This is fine if the boat doesn't do a flip-flop in the process. Under these conditions the skipper and crew must be ready to jump in any direction quickly, as the boat would just as soon capsize into the wind as with the wind, and frequently seems to have a suppressed desire to become a submarine. Under these conditions, illogical as it may sound at first, the centerboard should be up instead of down. The reason for this is that if the boat gets hit even slightly broadside by the breaking wave it will flip with the board down. If the board is up, it merely slides sideways and you have a chance of getting it aimed in the right direction again before it swaps ends.

Again, it is important to keep water out of the boat, so make sure the bailers are operating. If you know these conditions are going to exist before the start of the race put on your life jacket. (They used to be called Mae Wests, but since the bureaucrats now call them personal flotation devices, the name no longer seems appropriate.) Put the jackets on—their weight will help you balance the boat if you are wearing them, and they do not do any good stowed away in the boat. Also, as I have found from sad experience, they are hard to find and harder to put on after you have capsized.

On a broad reach with a centerboard boat, do not yield to the temptation to pull the centerboard up too far. A smooth board will have very little drag, and if the board is pulled up too high on a reach, the tendency of the boat to drift sideways will cause the board to be working at a very high angle of attack, and the drag will be increased over what it would have been with the board down a little farther. Also, on a run always leave enough of the board down in the water to keep the slot in the keel closed, unless you have proper flaps. Pulling the board all the way up lets water flow into the slot and increases drag instead of reducing it if your board is smooth. If it is rough and has square edges, pull it up. Pivot boards will sometimes jam if an attempt is made to lower them while on a reach in a good wind. Heading directly downwind and shaking the boat a little will generally free them. (Remember this if you are a dagger board man and are sailing a borrowed pivot board boat in a race.)

Develop a standard routine for each maneuver, such as putting on the boom vang prior to rounding a windward mark and raising the centerboard as the mark is being rounded. In developing these standard routines, remember to do things in the order of their importance as far as making the boat go fast. For example, setting the whisker pole or spinnaker has much more effect on the speed of the boat than adjusting draft in the mainsail.

A standard procedure can be worked out for other things also, such as jibing on a run, rounding marks, etc. Practice these so that you and the crew know what each of you is going to do and when. No matter how much you race, practicing this way is a good idea throughout the season—you simply cannot be good without practicing, no matter how smart you are. In close competition you may frequently have to act quickly, and you won't have time to tell your crew what to do. In these cases, practice will prevent bungling a maneuver.

After you have followed all of the suggestions that have been given above on how to get the most out of your boat and your sails, there is still one more thing to learn, and this will be the most difficult—that is to avoid the nautical equivalent of "buck fever." Many good skippers with good boats, when just playing around can keep up with the best, but they never succeed in placing high in official point-score races. Others who do very well in their own club point-score races will not do nearly as well as they should in big regattas. Curing this disease is very difficult. Probably the best cure is to have enough practice in sailing so that you have confidence in yourself and your equipment; then try to remain calm and take it easy while racing. I do not mean to suggest taking it easy to the extent of sailing a sloppy race, but I do recommend taking it easy to the extent of not worrying to the point where you start pressing too hard. There are times when this is easier said than done.

The best way to demonstrate the existence of this nautical equivalent of buck fever is to have a handicap race in which all of the boats are started at different times, their starts being timed so that theoretically they will all finish at the same time. The amount of time they are given on the start is determined from their previous performance in official races. The skippers who are really good but who fold up under pressure will generally finish far ahead of the time at which they should finish in the case of a handicap race with no one pressing them. A few races such as this are helpful in building up the morale of the less successful skippers—it shows them that if they would only relax, they would do a lot better.

PART III

Racing Tactics

1

General Principles of Starting

STARTING IS A VERY DIFFICULT SUBJECT TO DESCRIBE. I HAVE READ A NUMber of books and articles and none gives an exact formula; the reason is there is none. There are a number of pointers and techniques that can assist you but it takes experience to become a consistently good starter, and even the best ones don't get it right all the time. You have to develop a sense of timing, so the best advice is to jump right in and start learning.

One of the best ways to lose races is to leave the dock at the last minute and dash madly for the starting line, arriving a minute or so before the start. Under these conditions you generally arrive in a somewhat flustered condition and have no opportunity to get the feel of the boat under the conditions in which you will be racing, and you have no opportunity for last-minute adjustments on the sails. The best thing to do is to go out about an hour before the race and sail around for awhile to be sure that everything is working properly. This gives a final check on whether you have forgotten anything, and you can also at this time check to make sure you have the right sail combination and that they are set properly. This is the time to start making some judgments on probable wind shifts as well as velocity.

It is very desirable to have a wind velocity estimator, although the location at which you are checking the wind is frequently somewhat sheltered, and a certain amount of guesswork will be involved as to what the wind velocity is where you are going to race; and of course the wind usually changes after you get to the starting line. However, a wind velocity estimator will improve your guessing average greatly.

During hot weather along the coast the breeze over the water is likely to be much stronger during the hottest part of the day than it is over the land, and you will get badly fooled by calling the local airport for wind velocity. The wind along the shore near a large body of water in hot weather is made up of the normal surface wind, which is in the same direction but at a lower velocity than the upper-air wind, and the sea breeze which is caused by the air mass over the land being heated more than the air mass over the sea. The air mass over the land tends to rise, pulling in air from over the sea. This sea breeze apparently dissipates rapidly when it reaches the land, and when there is a strong on-shore breeze on a hot afternoon the wind velocity on the water may be as much as 10 or 15 miles an hour higher than the wind velocity given at an airport several miles inland. On inland lakes you can get fooled equally well in the other direction—the wind velocity on top of a control tower 75 feet above the ground at the airport may be lots more than the wind down on the water, particularly if the lake is surrounded by hills or trees. And regardless of where you are, it doesn't do any good to know what the wind is blowing 15 or 20 miles away at an airport, unless of course there is a front coming. I have seen La Guardia airport give 20 to 30 miles an hour and yet Larchmont remained a dead calm.

It is best to carry two stop watches, not only in case something happens to one of them but also so that you can take the time remaining yourself when you cross the line in the reverse direction and decide when you wish to come about for the actual start. The crew should watch so that he can start counting seconds about five seconds before you want to come about and to give you the time remaining until the gun goes off while you are heading for the line.

No matter how much experience you have in timing starts, remember to watch the flags. Check your time on each flag and gun, and particularly if you do not hear the starting gun, look for the flag signals on the committee boat. Arguing with a race committee is like arguing with a traffic cop—they are never wrong. And in the end, it is of academic interest only whether it was your timing or the race committee's timing that was actually wrong—the race committee is starting the race, and the flags count. So, make it a habit—even if you *know* your time is right and there are other boats ahead of you—to always look at the committee boat for the flag signals. If the recall flag is up and you have even the slightest suspicion that you might be early (ignoring your watch) go back and start over. You will lose only a few seconds, which is better than losing a race.

A good reason for reading the circular carefully when you are away from home is to be sure that you understand all the signals and can identify all the marks. Race committees at big regattas are very uncommunicative when they get on the water. When the signals for your race are hoisted, go over them with your crew to be sure that you have not made any mistake. Heading for the wrong mark or rounding it in the wrong direction can be very costly.

2

Starting to Windward

DURING THE TIME BETWEEN YOUR ARRIVAL NEAR THE STARTING LINE AND the actual start, make a careful check of the range through which the direction of the wind shifts, the frequency with which it shifts, and also determine whether most of the shifts are actual shifts or just apparent shifts due to increasing and decreasing wind velocity. About 15 minutes before the start re-check the tensions on the foot of your main and on the halyards. Take one last look around to be sure that everything is buttoned on tightly and then get ready for the start. Raise your board and check the rudder for weeds if there are any around. You will by this time know the direction that you can sail on both tacks, and you should now reach down the starting line and get the compass bearing of the starting line unless other classes are using it—in that case, project out beyond one end or the other. During all of the time up to your final approach to the line, keep an eye on the wind direction. Try a starboard tack close-hauled at least every 2 minutes and check your compass reading. A shift may make you revise your plans.

The installation of a compass should have been covered earlier under the subject of boat equipment, but there didn't seem to be a good place, and anyway many people think it is silly to put a compass on a small boat. It isn't—it's silly not to. Either a cheap airplane compass or an automobile compass is satisfactory, although good tactical compasses are made for sailboats. Neither will work at a very great angle of heel, but if you let the boat heel that much you aren't going anyplace anyway. The compass is very handy in trying to decide on which end of the line to start, but its greatest use will come up later. (There isn't as much skepticism on this subject as there once was.)

If the angle between the starboard tack close-hauled and the starting line is less than 45 degrees, the leeward end of the line will give a shorter course to the windward mark. If the line appears to be cockeyed, keep an eye on the committee boat—they can and sometimes do shift the line between the preparatory and warning guns, which may affect your starting plans. Also, in a high wind their anchor may drag which may result in a constantly shifting line. The 45-degree figure will be approximately correct for most small boats; it will be less for closer-winded larger boats.

If the wind is shifty, a fairly accurate last-minute check can be made, sailing parallel to the starting line watching whatever wind direction indicator you have. Unless the line is perfectly square to the wind, the indicator will be closer to parallel to the boat center-line when approaching one end of the line than it is when approaching the other end. The end towards which you are heading when the indicator is closest to parallel to the centerline is the favored end.

If you have neither a compass nor a wind direction indicator you can head the boat directly into the wind near the center of the line (if traffic will permit) and take a sight on both ends of the starting line. The end which is forward of the athwartship line of your boat is the favored end.

In general, when the leeward end of the line gives a better course to the windward mark, it is best to plan to start on the leeward end of the line, *providing you have practiced starts and can time them accurately.* A late start on the leeward end of the line is apt to be extremely bad because you will either have to follow other boats for some distance or try to work through the fleet on a port tack, which may be difficult. Incidentally, you have to be good and know what you are doing to start on the leeward end of the line on a port tack. No matter how clear that end of the line appears to be, a starboard tacker always seems to show up at the last minute to pick you off.

The only time that a port-tack start is safe is when it is impossible to cross the starting line on a starboard tack, and then be sure the race committee has not changed the line at the last minute (it ain't legal, but you are talking from the jail if they do and you get caught); keep your eyes open, and if you see trouble coming, avoid it before it arrives.

Sometimes special circumstances will exist which will make a start on the leeward end of the line inadvisable even if the course is favored from this end and you have confidence in your ability to time your start accurately. In case it will be necessary to tack soon after starting to clear an obstruction such as a shore line or breakwater, or if it is a very short beat to the windward mark, it is probably better to start at the windward end of the line even though the course is longer from this end, as you will have less interference when it is necessary to tack. Also, sometimes the wind, tide, or water conditions are such that an immediate shift to port tack is desirable. You may anticipate a clockwise shift in the wind, such as frequently happens on Long Island Sound in the afternoon when the wind is a light easterly, or there may be a strong head tide and the port tack will take you close to shore where the tide is less, or in a high wind you may want to go on a port tack to get close to a shore where the waves may not be so high. In these cases, the start should be made at the windward end of the line, even if the leeward end of the line gives a shorter distance.

The anti-barging rule has made the windward end of the line much more attractive for skippers accustomed to making well-timed, close-hauled starts, and it has also made this end of the line much less attractive for the boys who used to just hang around close to the line and then come in on a broad reach right with the gun. Barging itself is not illegal—if you can find a hole and sneak into it without interfering with anyone you are all right—but it's awfully risky business. The slightest interference with a close-hauled boat and you have no argument whatever—you are out. It is best not to try it.

In a light wind, stay close to the line so that wind shifts or a drop in the wind will not leave you waiting a long way away from the line. Keep your boat moving, and keep your wind clear all of the time that you are maneuvering around before the start in a light wind. Do not sit around just bouncing up and down, as it takes even a small boat a long time to get moving at maximum speed in a light wind once it has stopped or slowed down. Keep your eye on the wind pennant to be sure that the wind has not shifted without your noticing it. In a light, shifty wind it is particularly dangerous to hang around the leeward end of the line—stay away unless you have decided to start there.

The best tactics for starting will be determined by the size of the fleet in which you are starting. The old classic Vanderbilt timed start works well in a small fleet but needs to be modified for starting in a big fleet. However, its principles are basic so it will be described first in detail.

In timing your start, cross the line in the reverse direction to which the start will be made, and read the time remaining when you are even with the point on the line where you will cross it on the actual start, not at the point at which you cross the line in the reverse direction (Figure 8). Divide the remaining time by two and add to this half of the estimated time to jibe or tack. This amount of time should be determined by practice starts before the race. On small boats the amount added will vary from about 5 seconds in light winds to 2½ seconds with a wind of about 8 to 10 miles an hour to nothing with high winds. Adding nothing for tacking time in a high wind doesn't mean that the boat does not take some time to come about. It merely means that the boat goes faster on the beat for the line than it does on the reverse course, which is a very broad reach, and the jib is generally not working very effectively, which cancels out part or all of the time taken to tack or jibe. The proper time to hit the line in the reverse direction depends on the wind and the tactics that other boats are apparently going to use. In anything but a drifting match and in the absence of strong tides, the line should be crossed in the reverse direction at least 40 seconds before the start, but not more than a minute before. Larger boats of course require more time.

When approaching the line on the actual start, remember that you are crossing the line at an angle and that you must allow for that in estimating your position in relation to the line. There is a strong tendency to think you are closer than you actually are at the windward end of the line and farther away than you actually are at the leeward end (Figure 9).

This is the classic Vanderbilt start. In a small fleet it works well. However, with the large fleets usually encountered now, it is very difficult to use. The reason is that with a large fleet, boats will line up and reach back and forth on the line, creating a blanket of bad wind, and that will almost preclude a boat that is trying to get a good timed start from ever getting back to the line. It is not always such but it occurs often enough to preclude its use exclusively. Even if the blanket of bad air did not exist, you would still be confronted with a line of boats reaching down the line. You would have right of way over the windward boats but many skippers will ignore you until you hit them—and hitting another boat does slow you down. However, a timed start can be used in small fleets, and the technique can be used in the final approach to the line. In addition, practicing timed starts before the race gives you a feel for how far the boat will travel in the amount of wind on that day.

In large fleets it is frequently necessary to get to the line early in order to be able to find a place on the line. Starting in the second tier with disturbed air will seriously handicap a boat. In such

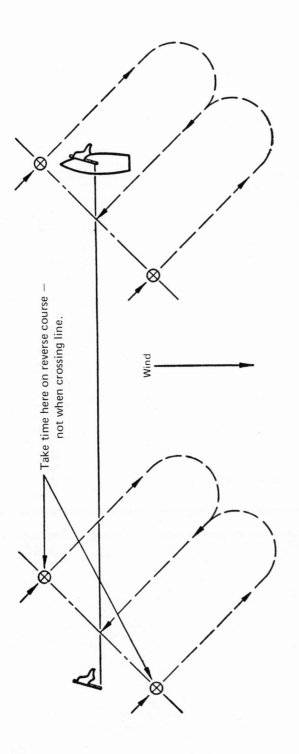

Take time here on reverse course — not when crossing line.

Wind

FIGURE 8

When crossing the starting line (or an extension of it) in order to time your start, you generally do not cross at the same spot at which you will actually cross the line on the start. If you do cross it at a different point, sight directly across the boat and read your watch when you are even with the point on the line at which you will cross it later.

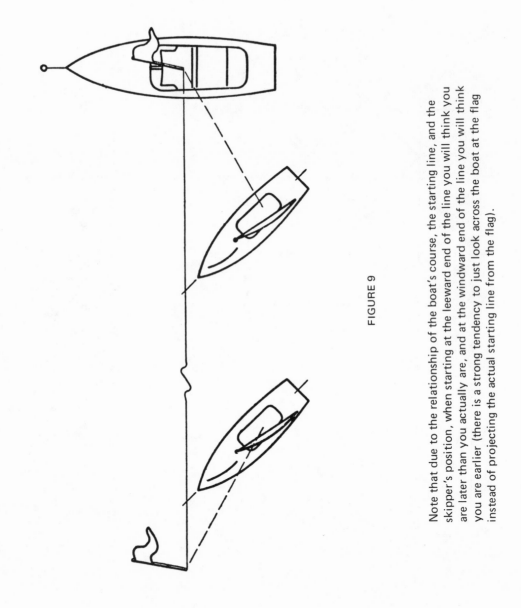

FIGURE 9

Note that due to the relationship of the boat's course, the starting line, and the skipper's position, when starting at the leeward end of the line you will think you are later than you actually are, and at the windward end of the line you will think you are earlier (there is a strong tendency to just look across the boat at the flag instead of projecting the actual starting line from the flag).

situations, the only use you can make of a timed start is to put you in the approximate location you think you ought to be. You have to plan on being early because the wall of disturbed air caused by boats already on the line can wreak havoc on the course and speed of a close-hauled boat. You have to learn the various methods of slowing your boat. You can reduce speed by cutting your power— that is, luffing your sails. Letting the jib flap, or backing the jib will slow you down but still leave some forward motion, enabling you to control direction. If you are still going too fast, luffing the main will further slow you down. Backing both the jib and the main is the most effective brake.

Finding a hole in a bunch of boats loafing down the line can sometimes best be accomplished by port tack reaching just below the line. When you find a hole you can tack to starboard just behind the last boat before the hole, thus putting you right on the line. At any rate, you should be moving fast enough to keep the boat to windward from running over you and taking your wind at the start or just afterwards. A bit of judicious luffing will usually persuade the windward boat to slow down. This will also open up a gap to your leeward and avoid your being backwinded by the boat to leeward. Again the goal is to have clear air and be accelerating when the gun goes. When there are a large number of boats reaching down a long starting line, it is amazing how often the boats in the middle of the parade are actually very far behind the line.

If it looks like the race is going to be a drifting match, plan your start early because with no wind you can't make much progress. With a large number of boats and a long starting line, it is of the greatest importance to pick the end of the line that will put you in a position to get the first puff of breeze when it comes. Picking the correct end of the line is largely guesswork, but probably the safest thing is to assume that if the wind has merely died a bit, it will come back from the same direction. If it is absolutely flat, play for a pronounced shift. When you start your final approach for the line, be sure that you are on a course that gives you right of way —be on the starboard tack close hauled if it is possible to cross the line on the starboard tack. With no wind, your ability to maneuver out of another boat's way is severely curtailed, and it is much better to let the other boat worry about keeping out of the way.

You will probably have no opportunity to time a practice start under these conditions as there is too much chance of getting left on the wrong side of the line. Stay on the right side of the line close to the position where you have decided to make your start. Try to estimate your speed in relation to the starting mark, and don't wait too long before heading for the line. I have headed for the line from a distance of 50 feet three minutes before the start and still been late.

A strong tide will have a great influence on the timing of your start. If the tide is against you, it will take you much longer to get back to the line than it did to reach from the line to the place where you tacked to make your start. Also—the tide will have a big effect on the course that you can actually make good. With a strong head tide and light wind, it may be difficult or even impossible to clear a large committee boat on the leeward end of the line, especially if it is moored to a buoy and if you happen to be blanketed a little. If the committee boat is on the windward end of the line it will simplify the problems involved in getting across the line, but in either case, with a light wind and a strong head tide, always hit the windward end of the line. Be late if necessary, but be right at the windward end. If your start happens to be timed perfectly you can just keep going or tack if you wish. If it doesn't turn out that way and you are following other boats, you can go onto a port tack and get clear at any time. Just the opposite rule applies with a light wind and a strong following tide. In this case, stay farther away from the line while maneuvering for the start, and take the leeward end unless the other end is far superior. If you must take the windward end, be sure you don't turn out to be barging at the last instant just because you did not allow enough for the effect of the tide (Figures 10 and 11).

Occasionally you will get starting lines going to windward when one end of the line is so much better than the other that you (and most of the others too) will have to start on the best end or take too much of a sacrifice. You know there will be an awful mob scene, so the problem is to make a start that is safe and as good as possible.

In the case where the windward end of the line is much the better, you want to cross the line as close to the windward end as possible, yet not take any chance of barging or being luffed above the mark. Also, you don't want to get caught much to leeward of the end of the line, as you will be hopelessly blanketed and you won't be able to go onto a port tack until about all the windward boats have passed you. If there are many boats in the race, you can't plan on timing your start by crossing the line in the reverse direction just before the start because the mob of boats approaching the line will look like the thundering herd in an old Western movie.

The thing to do is to get your bearing for the starboard tack, then sail the reverse course crossing the line right at the wind-

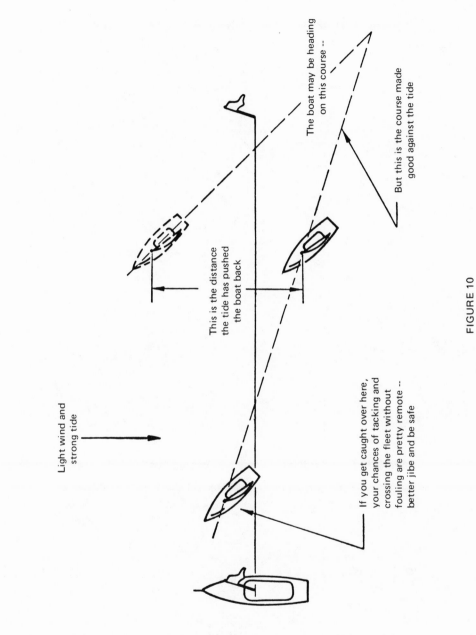

The boat may be heading on this course --

But this is the course made good against the tide

This is the distance the tide has pushed the boat back

Light wind and strong tide

If you get caught over here, your chances of tacking and crossing the fleet without fouling are pretty remote -- better jibe and be safe

FIGURE 10

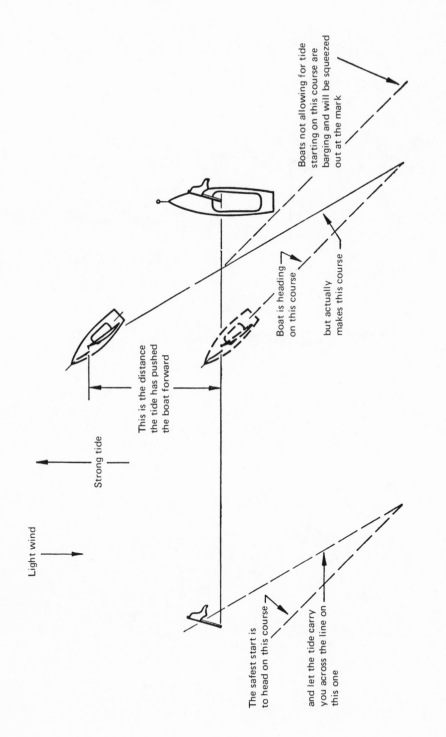

FIGURE 11

ward end sometime before the start when the congestion isn't too great. Sail back from the line for a minute or so until you can get a line on something by which you hope you can locate the same spot later—a house and a tree on shore, some stakes or buoys, or if you are starting a long way offshore, a guessed-at distance back of the line. Remember the amount of time it took you to get there and during the remaining maneuvering time, practice trying to get back to that spot. On the final run for the line, try to hit that spot just a few seconds later than you think you should, starboard tack, close-hauled, and going at top speed. This won't give you a perfect start, but if you are the third or fourth boat over and right at the windward end, you are doing all right. If there are any bargers, just keep going. If they don't know the rules yet, they might as well learn them then and there (Figure 12).

The other case is where it is just barely possible to cross the line on a starboard tack. In this case, you will again not be able to time a start by sailing a reverse course just before the gun, because everyone will be in the same place at the same time. After getting your starboard-tack course, take the time required to sail on a starboard tack, close-hauled from a point even with the windward end of the line to the place where you will cross the line near the leeward end and note how far you are behind the mark on the windward end of the line when sailing this course. Plan your start to arrive even with the windward end of the line, at the correct distance back of the windward end, between 5 and 10 seconds later than you think you should in order to hit the leeward end exactly right. The reason for this 5-to-10-second margin is that a leeward boat might luff you a little and force you closer to the line than you would like to be. There will probably be some misguided souls who will be trying to hit this end of the line on a port tack. Yell as loudly as you can as it will only slow you down if you hit them (Figure 13).

The advantages of these methods of starting when the lines are as illustrated are that you are assured of at least a fairly good start and freedom to tack soon after crossing the line, and also you tack or jibe to start your final beat to the line in an area that is not congested with boats; therefore there is less chance of fouling anyone when tacking or jibing, and less chance of being prevented by other boats from tacking or jibing when you wish to. These starts are of particular value when the wind is tricky and likely to shift at any time. They assure you of being relatively free to tack in case of a shift soon after the start. Also, poor starting lines such as we are discussing here usually happen as a result of tricky winds—it would be very seldom that a race committee would pur-

STARTING ON THE WINDWARD END OF THE LINE
WHEN THIS END HAS A BIG ADVANTAGE

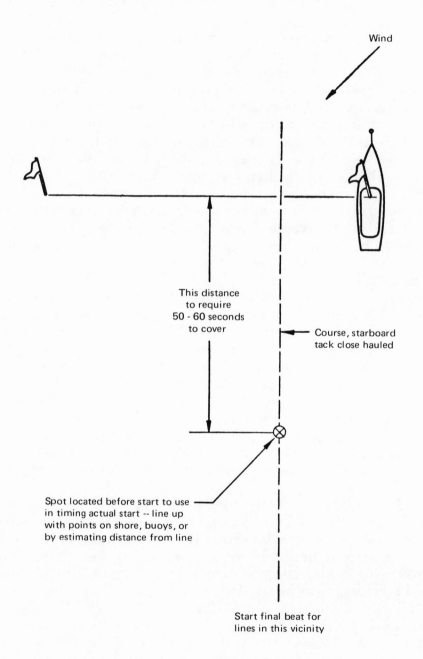

Wind

This distance
to require
50 - 60 seconds
to cover

Course, starboard
tack close hauled

Spot located before start to use
in timing actual start -- line up
with points on shore, buoys, or
by estimating distance from line

Start final beat for
lines in this vicinity

FIGURE 12

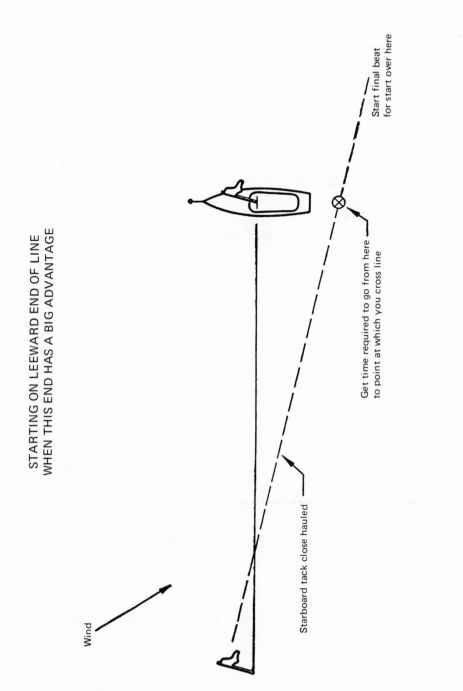

STARTING ON LEEWARD END OF LINE
WHEN THIS END HAS A BIG ADVANTAGE

Wind

Starboard tack close hauled

Get time required to go from here
to point at which you cross line

Start final beat
for start over here

FIGURE 13

posely lay out a line giving so much advantage to one end.

When starting at the windward end of the line under these circumstances, you can often hit the line 10 seconds late at full speed and have clear air. The early boats have been braking to slow down and some have been barging and have been wiped out by the committee boat.

With a small light boat which accelerates quickly, a skillful skipper can make what I call a stalled start under these circumstances. He simply parks his boat a little to windward and behind the spot where he wants to be at the start, sails flapping and with little or no headway. This method of starting requires a keen sense of timing to decide when to start moving in order to not get left at the starting gate, but with a boat which will accelerate quickly it will work. It can be done with Snipes but requires an extremely fine combination of luck and skill.

3

Starts Off the Wind

RACE COMMITTEES SHOULD BE LINED UP AND SHOT FOR STARTING A RACE off the wind, particularly if the start is running before the wind. Sometimes, however, it is impossible, as in the case of clubs that have fixed starting marks. Also, it is normal for cruising boats to have fairly long courses and they usually start in the direction of the first mark, no matter what the wind direction.

Regardless of the distance between the ends of the starting line and the first mark, be very cautious in deciding on a start on the leeward end of the line when starting on a reach. A start on the leeward end is safe only if the wind is strong and steady and if your start is timed perfectly. Even if the wind is strong and steady and if it appears that the leeward end of the line will be relatively free from boats so that you can get an accurately timed start, it will still probably pay to start on the leeward end only if this end has a big advantage as far as distance is concerned or if this end will put you on the inside at the next mark and the next mark is fairly close.

If there aren't too many boats, the best start is to approach the windward end of the line close-hauled. In this way you have the right of way and have a great deal of freedom on the point at which you cross the starting line. If there is a large number of boats in the race, you may have difficulty defending your right of way and may get hit by a number of windward boats—all of whom you can disqualify if you can remember their numbers, and whom you can theoretically get to pay for the damage to your boat—but you can't do anything about the poor start you will end up with after being fouled.

In light airs it is almost never safe to make a start on the leeward end of the line when the starting course is a reach. No matter how well-timed your start is, you are almost sure to get bottled up. In light shifty winds when starting off the wind, it is frequently better to stay behind the line, keeping your boat moving fast and starting a little late near the center or the windward end, locating a clear spot and heading for it; it is much better to hit the line late and going fast than to hit it on time and be blanketed by other boats. If you do get bottled up on a start of this type, it is frequently better to cut behind a lot of boats and try to get upwind of them, rather than to stay in the middle of the mess even though you go a long way out of your way going behind boats to get up-wind.

In starting a race where the first leg is directly before the wind, don't do the obvious thing and start directly before the wind. A broad reach is much faster than a run before the wind, and in addition, if you are reaching you will automatically be the leeward boat and have the right of way. The only time this is a poor idea is when there is a large number of boats starting and most of them haven't thought about starting on a reach. I tried it in Dallas one year with 36 boats in the race. It sounded like at least 18 of them hit me while I was trying to get unscrambled after a windward boat rammed me just ahead of the transom and headed me up into an involuntary luffing match with several other boats about two seconds before the gun went off (Figure 14).

When the wind is light and fluky, a good downwind start is not particularly important as those behind generally blanket those ahead promptly after the start anyway. Unless you find a good clear place right at the start, you are just as well off to start a little late, with clear wind.

When the wind is steady, there is a good chance that practically everyone will arrive at the first mark at the same time after a downwind start. It is therefore a good idea to pick the end of the line that will put you on the inside at the mark, especially if the course is fairly short.

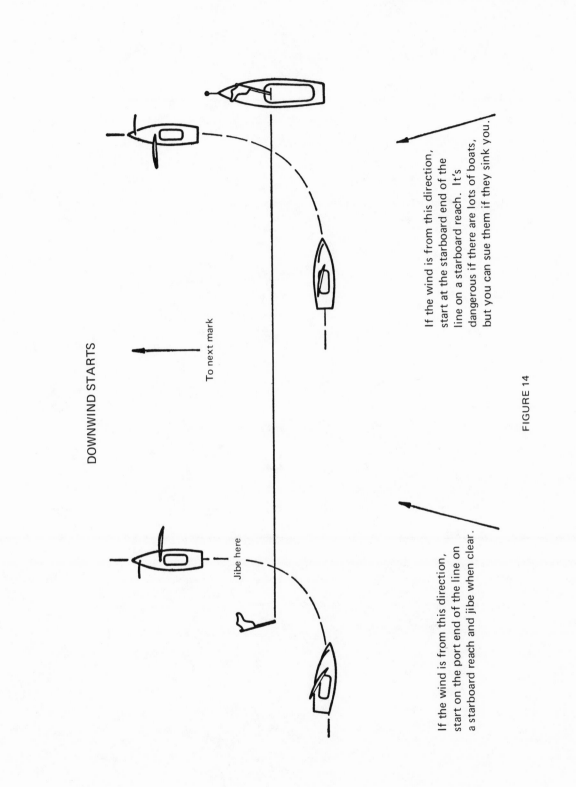

DOWNWIND STARTS

To next mark

Jibe here

If the wind is from this direction, start at the starboard end of the line on a starboard reach. It's dangerous if there are lots of boats, but you can sue them if they sink you.

If the wind is from this direction, start on the port end of the line on a starboard reach and jibe when clear.

FIGURE 14

4

Beating to Windward

IMMEDIATELY TO LEEWARD OF ANY BOAT AND EXTENDING FOR A DISTANCE of about three mast lengths, there is a wind shadow where the wind velocity is greatly decreased. To leeward of the boat, except right at the bow, behind the boat, and even behind and slightly to windward, there is a region where the wind direction is noticeably changed and the velocity is slightly reduced. To leeward of the bow of the boat there is a very small region where the direction of the wind is deflected opposite to the normal deflection and where the velocity is accelerated slightly (Figure 15).

A boat immediately to leeward of the bow of another boat and slightly ahead of it is said to be in the safe leeward position and will be able to forge ahead of the windward boat. This is true, however, only if the boats are very close together and if the mast of the leeward boat is approximately even with the bow of the windward boat; otherwise, a boat which is to leeward of another boat, behind another boat, or even slightly to windward and behind is in a hopeless position, and it is practically impossible to work past the leading boat from this position. Dr. Curry was the first author to call attention to the "safe leeward position," and it really works—but there are a lot of ifs, wheres, and buts about it. Theoretically the leeward yacht has the advantage when its bow is even with that of the windward one, but in practice that is cutting it too close. In the safe leeward position, the leeward boat has the advantage for two reasons—the slight acceleration and favorable deflection of the wind in the vicinity of the jib of the windward boat is favorable to the leeward boat, and also the decel-

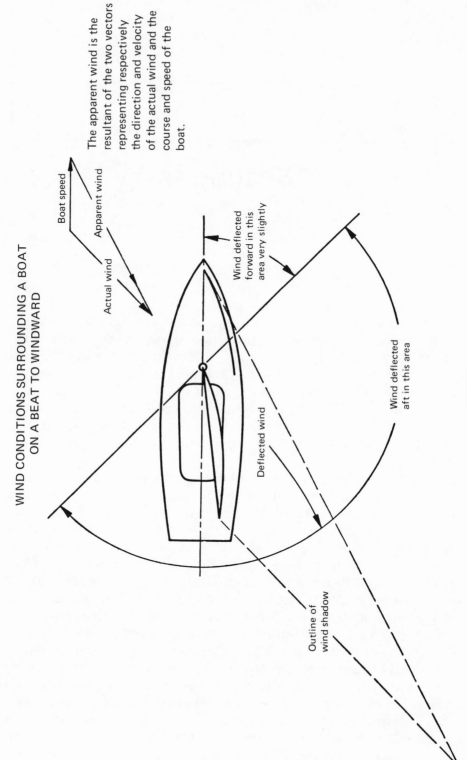

WIND CONDITIONS SURROUNDING A BOAT
ON A BEAT TO WINDWARD

The apparent wind is the resultant of the two vectors representing respectively the direction and velocity of the actual wind and the course and speed of the boat.

Boat speed

Apparent wind

Actual wind

Wind deflected forward in this area very slightly

Wind deflected aft in this area

Deflected wind

Outline of wind shadow

FIGURE 15

eration and unfavorable deflection of the wind by the mainsail of the leeward boat is very bad for the windward boat.

The hopeless leeward position is hopeless because the wind velocity of the leeward or following boat is somewhat decreased, and also the deflection of the wind is such that the following or leeward boat cannot point as high. Except in the direct wind shadow the deflection of the wind is more important than the decrease in wind velocity, as the decrease in velocity is very slight except in the immediate shadow of the sails of the windward boat.

Because of this wind deflection, a boat on the opposite tack cutting behind another boat will be able to point appreciably higher than it normally would be able to point. A starboard tack boat must not take advantage of this lift by altering course to pick off a port-tack boat which was clearing the starboard tacker before the latter altered course (Figure 16).

When several boats on port tack are working their way through a group on starboard tack, it frequently becomes evident that there is still quite a bit of misunderstanding of the rules pertaining to the rights of a leeward yacht approaching an obstruction when the obstruction is another yacht racing and having the right of way. Most of the misunderstanding comes from not reading the rules carefully. The important points are that the leeward yacht can hail when safe piloting requires action by the leeward boat, and if she intends to tack, cannot do so without colliding with the other yacht. Figure 17 illustrates this.

There is also some misunderstanding concerning the giving of room at obstructions when the obstruction is another yacht racing, having right of way. Everyone knows about giving room at marks, but they sometimes forget about giving room where the obstruction is another yacht racing which has right of way. Figure 18 illustrates this.

If you are bottled up on a windward start, get clear as soon as possible. If it is necessary to cut through part of the fleet on a port tack, do not worry about having to go behind a bunch of starboard tackers. Bear off, slack the sheets slightly, shoot under their stern, and then head up immediately after passing. You will be surprised how often the spurt that you get from bearing off and being able to head up a little higher after passing will enable you to take the starboard tacker the next time. In any case, it is a good general principle to follow to never crowd your luck by trying to pass in front of a starboard tacker. If you are not absolutely sure, either come about or go behind him. In case of an argument, the race committee will decide, and rightly, that the starboard tacker is right.

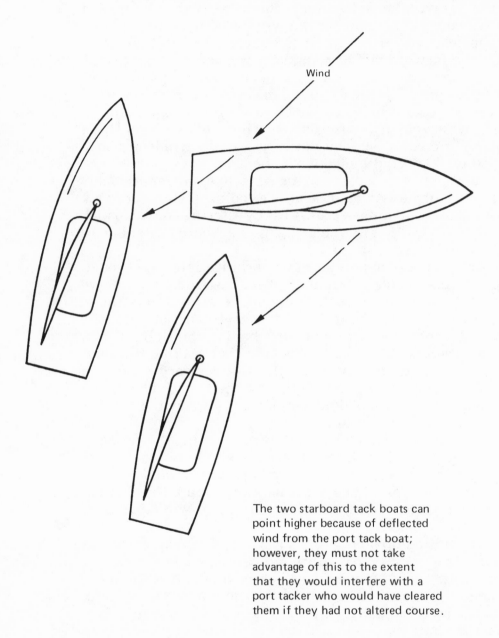

Wind

The two starboard tack boats can
point higher because of deflected
wind from the port tack boat;
however, they must not take
advantage of this to the extent
that they would interfere with a
port tacker who would have cleared
them if they had not altered course.

FIGURE 16

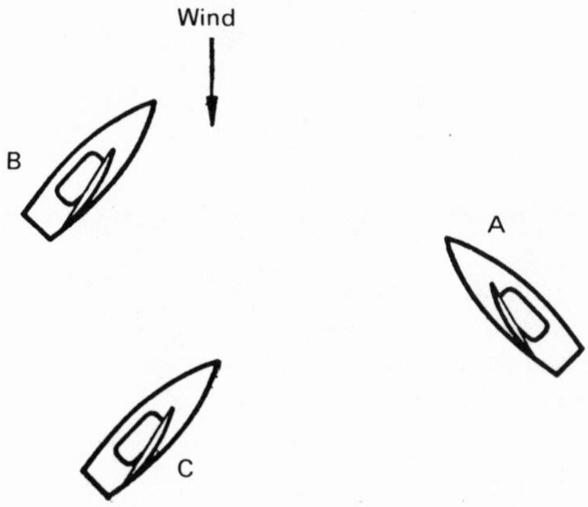

Wind

B

Safe piloting requires C to take action. C cannot hail B about because C can tack and clear B without a collision, going behind B. If C does hail B, B can respond "you tack." C must then tack and if B does not interfere there is no argument.

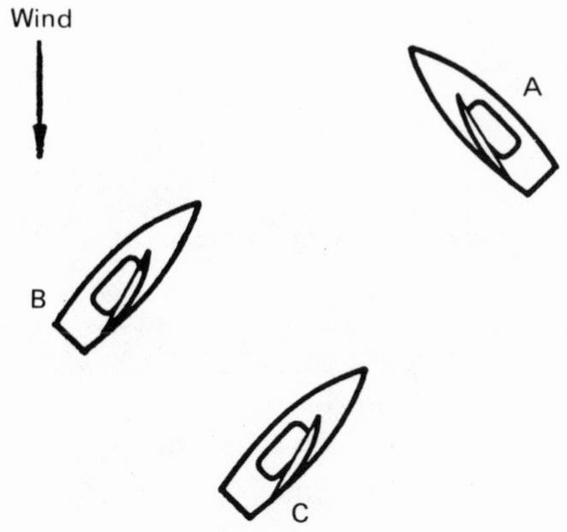

C

Wind

A

B

Safe piloting does not require any action by C so she cannot hail B about.

C

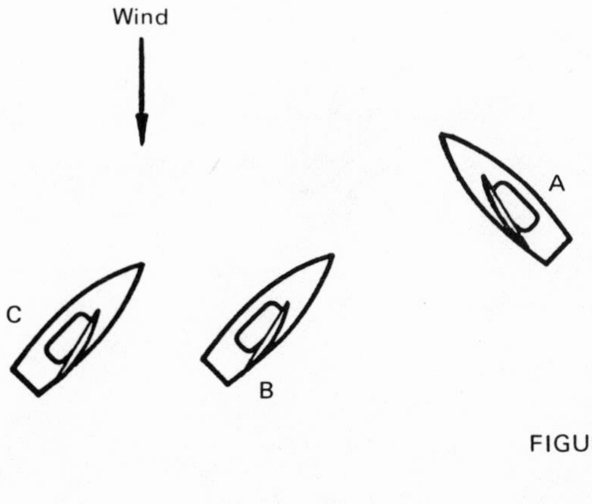

Wind

A

Safe piloting requires B to take action. If she decides to tack, C would have to come about upon a hail by B.

C

B

FIGURE 17

Wind

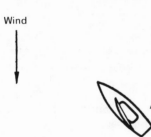

B can clear A by going astern, but must also allow C room to clear, as A is an obstruction, being another yacht racing, having right of way.

Wind

At Position $A_1B_1C_1$, B could hail C about. The skipper of B, however, decides to go behind A. When he do so, he must give C room to clear A also.

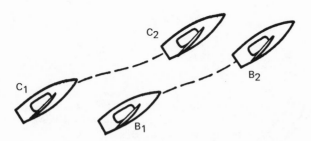

FIGURE 18

Tacking only a few feet under another boat to get a safe lee-ward position requires close calculation. Your boat loses speed as it tacks (the smaller the boat, the more speed it loses), and you must tack far enough ahead so that you can pick up full speed after tacking before the other boat puts you in his shadow. In general, it will only work if you had *almost* room to have crossed in front of the other boat. If you are this close, it is probably worth a try. There are, of course, special circumstances where it is very desir-able to try it. The one situation in which it should *always* be tried is when you are close to a mark which is to be left to port and you are on a port tack with a starboard tacker approaching and you are sure he can lay the mark. Then you have nothing to lose by trying for a safe leeward position. But if he cannot lay the mark, or if the mark is to be left to starboard, *never* try it unless you have room to tack directly in front of him. If you do not have this much room, go behind him and tack about one and one-half lengths to wind-ward of him. When you do this, he then cannot tack for the mark without interfering with you. Figure 19 shows what may happen from here on, depending on who thinks fastest.

All winds shift somewhat in direction no matter what size body of water you are on. They merely shift less often and through a smaller range on large bodies of water than they do on small ones, except in the case of very light winds, and then no rules hold anywhere.

Figure 20 shows how only a very slight shift will alter the relative positions of two boats on opposite tacks. It is for this rea-son that it is necessary to detect wind shifts and tack with them unless some special circumstances make it undesirable to do so. In detecting wind shifts, a compass is indispensable even on a small body of water. Many skippers formerly were scornful of using a compass for this purpose—they did not need one; they could watch their course in relation to a tree on the shore, a buoy, or other boats, and detect wind shifts that way. Maybe they could, but I wasn't that smart—and sometimes they weren't either. I used to be able to pick up lots of places on a beat after getting bottled up in a bad start just by catching the wind shifts that others either did not detect or ignored. Things are lots tougher now with more com-passes in use.

Frequently the wind will be from a slightly different direction on one end of the beat than it is on the other. This very often happens when the course comes close to shore or a bend in a river or lake—the wind tends to blow perpendicular to the shore. If you have found this out by sailing around beforehand or if you have detected it during the first lap of the two-lap race, take your first

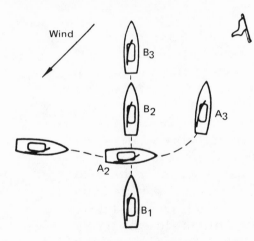

When B cannot lay the mark and A is not far enough ahead to try for a safe leeward position, A should go behind B and tack so as to be about one and one-half boat lengths to windward of B. B then cannot tack for the mark until A does.

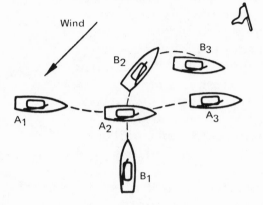

However, if the skipper of B is smart, as soon as A is under his stern, he will tack. He may fall behind A because A will be going faster, but if the mark is close, he can still probably prevent A from tacking until he tacks himself.

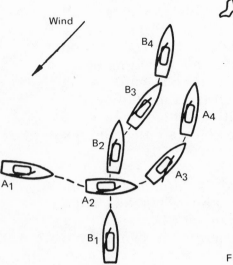

But if the skipper of A is still smarter, he will watch B and the instant that B starts to tack, he will tack (it's a good idea to hail too). Study U.S.Y.R.U. Appeal Decision 129 before trying this. There are some limitations.

FIGURE 19

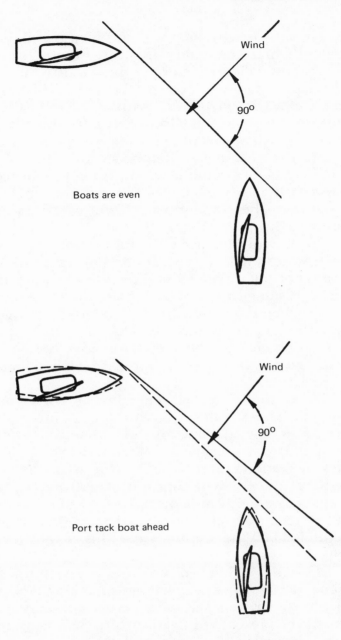

Boats are even

Port tack boat ahead

FIGURE 20

The effect of the shift is compounded by the fact that one boat points higher by the amount of the shift, while the other points lower by the same amount. If we assume the wind shifts 5°, stays there 2½ minutes, and then shifts back, a boat which tacked with both shifts will gain 250 feet in 5 minutes on one which ignored them, both boats being assumed to be making 4 miles an hour.

tack from the start or from the leeward mark in the direction toward which the wind will shift (Figure 21).

Light winds are generally more shifty than high ones, and in light winds there will usually be no waves to interfere with tacking, and it will pay to tack with every shift. Before tacking, however, be sure that the wind is actually shifting and that the shift is not just an apparent one from the wind velocity dropping momentarily. A compass is helpful in finding out quickly whether the wind has gone around with you when you tacked, as it sometimes does, particularly when you have tacked on an apparent shift, as sometimes these apparent shifts precede an actual shift in the opposite direction (Figure 22).

Shifts will also occur in high winds but usually not as frequently, nor will they shift through as great an angle. In high winds and big waves, more time is lost tacking than in light winds, and it is sometimes difficult to decide whether it will pay to tack or not when the wind shifts. Generally it will not unless the shift is quite definite. If the wind has definitely shifted against you, however, you had better tack quickly—the wind is likely to stay from the new direction for some time when it does definitely shift in a high wind.

Occasionally you will encounter a persistent shift in the last part of a beat. It will start as a slight lift but continue to lift. If you are to the leeward side of the course, you cannot help but lose ground. If you continue to ride the lift you may end up having to tack back to the mark, usually after many boats have rounded. If you feel the lift will continue it will pay to cut your losses by tacking and gain some distance toward the middle of the course before tacking back. You will still lose ground but not as much as if you held on the original tack. This is known as tacking into the wheel.

If you know that you can't beat the boats ahead of you on speed alone, it may pay to experiment in a long tack. If the wind shifts in your favor, you may pick up several places. If it doesn't shift, you haven't lost anything. If it shifts against you, you gambled and lost. Conversely, if you are fairly confident of doing well with just ordinary breaks, always go to the windward mark in a series of fairly short tacks. Come about on every shift, and if the wind doesn't shift for quite awhile, come about anyway before you get too far away from the middle of the fleet. If there are a lot of boats closely bunched ahead of you, the exact middle may not be a good choice as the wind is likely to be very disturbed. Going to either side far enough to get clear air will pay.

A windward leg which runs parallel to a shore line is particu-

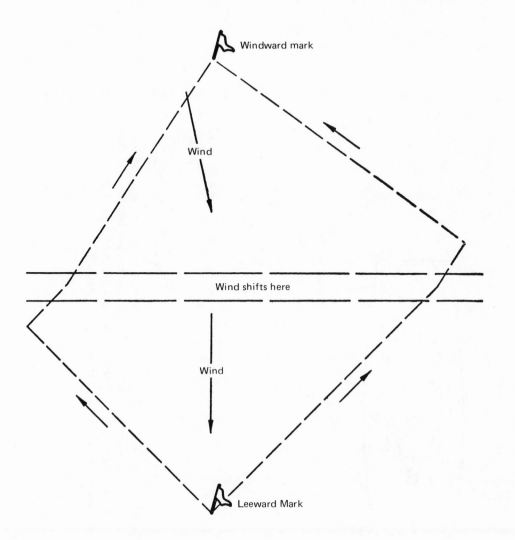

The condition shown above will frequently occur in the vicinity of a storm, on a lake near a point or a bend in the lake, or on a large body of water when the course is more or less at right angles to the shore. In the example shown, assuming the windward leg to be a mile long and the wind to shift as shown, the boat leaving the leeward mark on the starboard tack would beat the other one to the windward mark by 1000 feet!

FIGURE 21

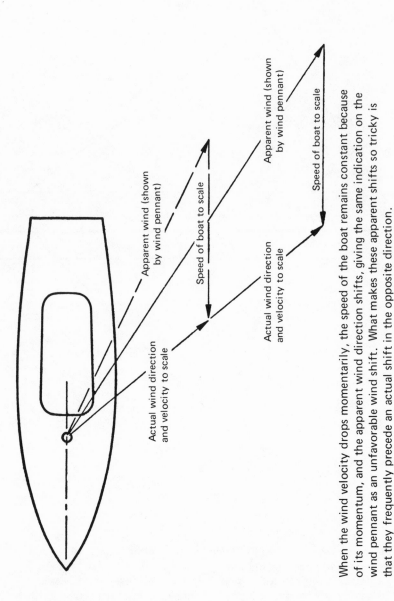

Apparent wind (shown by wind pennant)

Speed of boat to scale

Actual wind direction and velocity to scale

Apparent wind (shown by wind pennant)

Speed of boat to scale

Actual wind direction and velocity to scale

FIGURE 22

When the wind velocity drops momentarily, the speed of the boat remains constant because of its momentum, and the apparent wind direction shifts, giving the same indication on the wind pennant as an unfavorable wind shift. What makes these apparent shifts so tricky is that they frequently precede an actual shift in the opposite direction.

larly tricky. About the only way to find out whether it is a good idea to go close to a shore is to either try it yourself, or keep a close eye on someone else. Sometimes you don't dare go near a shore line, and at other times you don't dare not to. Usually you cannot point as high on approaching a shore as you could out away from the shore, but after tacking you will be able to point higher for awhile. Generally the safest thing to do is to take short tacks, not approaching the shore too closely until someone else does. Then watch him carefully and act according to the results he is getting.

If the wind happens to shift while you are close to shore so that you can sail a course straight to the mark parallel to the shore, don't be too jubilant, especially if the banks are high along the shore. This shift means that the wind is now crossing the shore line and anything may happen. Generally you can point higher, but sometimes the wind speed drops to the point where you lose more than you gain. Watch boats farther off shore carefully, and if they are moving faster, the quicker you swallow your pride and get away from the shore the better—even if you make what appears to be an unnecessary tack in order to get farther out, or bear off so that you will have to tack back later.

In tacking close to another boat don't assume that the rules let you tack as you please. They don't, in spite of the fact that quite a few skippers apparently think so. Remember the other boat need not anticipate the necessity of clearing you. He can hold his course until you have completed your tack. (See definition of tacking in the IYRU racing rules.) At that time, he must *start* to clear you, and you can't expect him to have a helicopter attachment to do it. And—don't forget—if you are the leeward of two port-tack boats and are going over to starboard tack, yell loud enough for anyone within a hundred feet to hear you—*before* you tack. Figure 23 illustrates the practical application of this rule.

Covering is done by staying on the same tack as another boat and either directly ahead or ahead and to windward. On a beat this is very effective, as it slows down the other boat and makes it fall off so that it cannot point as high. This effect only extends to about three mast lengths from the boat; however, if you are ahead, it always pays to cover your most dangerous competitor. Even if you are far enough ahead (four or five boat lengths) so that you are not interfering with his wind, it is still desirable to stay on the same tack so that he cannot get the benefit of a wind shift which you do not get.

However, do not waste time covering another boat which you know will beat you eventually. It is not only a poor way to win friends and influence people, but the inevitable tacking duel will

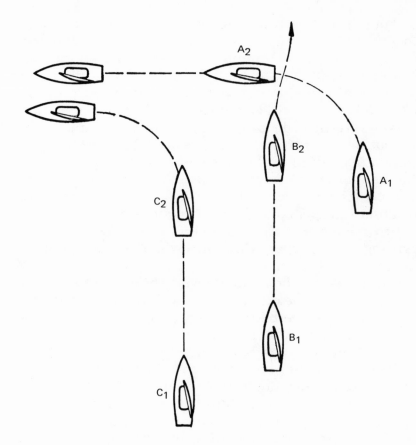

FIGURE 23

A commences to tack at A, and while he is not required to hail, it is a good idea to do so anyway as he may be disqualified if a collision occurs and he did not hail. A completes tack at A_2. At this time the other yachts must start to clear A. They do not need to anticipate the necessity of clearing A. B_1 and C_1 are the closest positions in which other yachts may be when A is at Position A_1 and still hold their courses to Positions B_2 and C_2 before starting to clear A. B bears off slightly and C tacks. Note that in the case of B, which is one boat length to windward of A, A must be clear ahead by one and one-quarter boat lengths when starting to tack. In the case of C, which is far enough to windward so that she will have to tack to clear A (two or more boat lengths to windward), A must be two boat lengths clear ahead. These distances are not necessarily exactly correct for any particular type of boat, but they illustrate the absolute minimum clearances that must be allowed. More is recommended to avoid being protested.

cost you time which you cannot afford to lose as your own nearest competitor is probably merrily sailing along without any interference and will soon be hopelessly ahead of you. Of course if you are unfortunate enough to have won any kind of championship, you are fair game for everyone, and you can anticipate being covered by anyone within 150 feet.

When another boat tacks to cover you, the safest thing to do is to go over to the opposite tack while he is tacking, unless there are other boats around that you can't clear, or you are already fetching the mark and another tack would make you overstand it. If these circumstances exist, all you can do is make the best of a bad situation. If the other boat has crossed in front of you and tacked, slack your sheets and bear off a little and hope you get through his wind shadow before he picks up speed after tacking. Of course, if he is smart he will bear off too—it's legal under the rules for a close-hauled boat to bear off on another close-hauled boat to leeward, although of course the windward boat must not touch the leeward one—but the windward boat generally doesn't notice the leeward one bearing off, and sometimes you can break through (Figure 24).

If the covering boat tacks to leeward of you and far enough ahead to get a safe leeward position and you don't want to split tacks, there isn't anything much you can do. If you aren't already laying the mark, you can try to split tacks when you are clear of other boats, but it probably won't do any good as the other boat will tack to cover you. If the two of you are well ahead, you can try to split tacks and if the other boat tacks to cover you, overstand the mark on purpose; then after tacking for the mark, bear off and try to go through to leeward. However, generally the best thing to do under these circumstances is just to relax and wait to get to the mark.

When trying to break through to windward of a boat which has tacked under you for a safe leeward position, remember that as soon as he has completed his tack, he has the right of way and you may have trouble keeping clear of him if his safe leeward position works. Don't wait too long to do something when you find that he has a safe leeward on you. If you tack soon enough, you may get clear. If you don't, you will have to luff in order to keep clear of him until you have dropped back astern of him (Figure 25).

There is one place where pinching is good tactics. This is in case you are fairly well ahead of another boat, but to leeward. In this case you are not causing him much trouble, and you cannot tack without interfering with him. This is a good time to do a little judicious pinching—not too much—but enough to work up to where you are directly in front of him. He will, of course, be going

BREAKING THROUGH TO LEEWARD OF A BOAT TACKING TO COVER

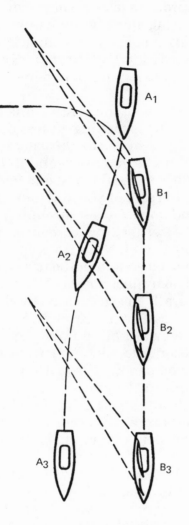

FIGURE 24

B_1 has completed her tack just enough ahead of A_1 so A_1 can clear B_1.
A starts to bear off as soon as it is obvious that B will tack in front of
A and slightly to windward. The critical point is at Position A_2B_2
where A is directly in the wind shadow of B. If A can pick up enough
speed by slacking sheets and bearing off while B is regaining speed lost
in tacking to break through at Position A_2B_2, he will soon be clear as
at A_3B_3. When this maneuver fails, it is generally because A was too
far behind B at Position A_1B_1, or because A did not bear off far enough
at Position A_2B_2. It is a difficult maneuver to perform successfully.

BREAKING THROUGH TO WINDWARD OF A BOAT TACKING TO COVER

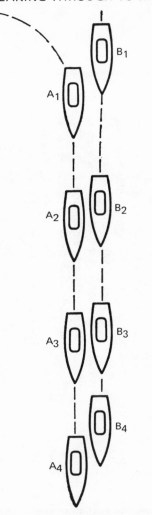 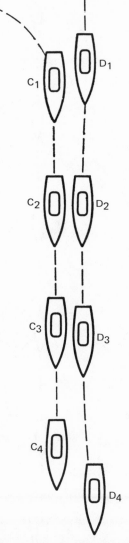

A_1 and C_1 have completed tacks under B_1 and D_1, hoping to get safe leeward positions. About all that B and D can do is to sail their boats as fast as possible and be sure to keep clear of A and C which have right of way, including luffing rights. At B_2, B should realize that he is not going to make it. He will hold his own for a short while, then start to fall back. Unless there are good reasons for not tacking, he should do so. At D_2, D has gotten up to where his bow is even with that of C. If D can gain a trifle more as at D_3, C is through.

FIGURE 25

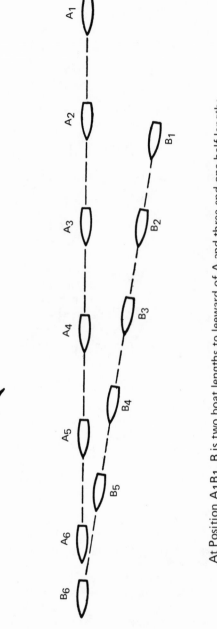

At Position A_1B_1, B is two boat lengths to leeward of A and three and one-half lengths ahead, but cannot safely tack for the mark as A is on a starboard tack and B would not be able to tack and cross in front of A. B, therefore, starts pinching a little (the amount shown in the illustration is exaggerated), sacrificing some of the lead over A in order to work to windward. If the skipper of A is smart, he will start pinching too, but he usually doesn't realize what is going on until about Position A_4B_4, by which time it is too late. Even if A then starts to pinch, all he can accomplish is hold about the same course as he has been sailing, as at A_5B_5 and A_6B_6. B is backwinding A badly.

FIGURE 26

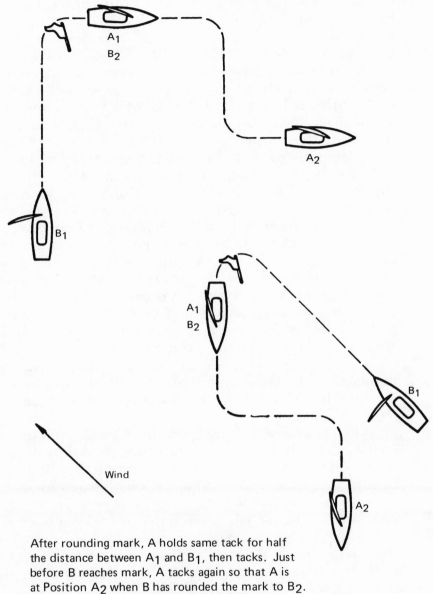

After rounding mark, A holds same tack for half
the distance between A_1 and B_1, then tacks. Just
before B reaches mark, A tacks again so that A is
at Position A_2 when B has rounded the mark to B_2.
If B tacks immediately after rounding mark, A
tacks at the same time to cover.

FIGURE 27

faster than you for a while, but as you get closer he will slow down and when you get directly ahead of him, he's through. (If he has his eyes open and recognizes what you are doing, he will start pinching, too—but usually he doesn't realize what is going on until it is too late.) (Figure 26)

If you are only a fairly short distance ahead of your most dangerous competitor, always stay on the same tack regardless of wind shifts. If it is toward the end of a regatta and he is the only one who can beat you, stay on the same tack with him and cover him no matter how crazy you think he is. If you are well ahead of him (over ten boat lengths), it is not necessary to stay on the same tack. Pick up your tacks according to the wind shifts, but always stay between him and the mark. Don't ever let him get off by himself where he might pick up a breeze that you do not get.

If you are covered by a boat which you know you can beat, do everything possible to get clear, but do not get excited and start overstanding marks or pinching the boat in the process. If the wind is shifty and you are covered by a skipper who is good at catching the wind shifts and it is early in the race, the best thing to do is to just resign yourself to being covered for the time being and wait to get clear later. If you are covered late in a race, occasionally a false tack—that is going halfway about and then coming back to the original tack—will work. If this doesn't work, try to maneuver your tacking so that you end up directly to leeward of the covering boat, then bear off a little and try to sail through his lee.

When rounding a mark going onto a beat, and there is another boat behind that you want to cover, remember that when he rounds the mark you must be on the same tack he is. If he is close behind you, either jibe at the mark or harden up on the wind as the case may be, but do not tack until he does. If far enough ahead, you can do a better job of covering by tacking once shortly after rounding the mark, then tacking back before your competitor rounds the mark. Be sure to make your second tack soon enough to be able to tack again if your competitor tacks immediately on rounding the mark (Figure 27).

If your competitor is very close behind you as you round the mark onto a beat, don't let him suck you into cutting close to the mark as you approach it. If you do, he can bear off a bit before getting to the mark and cut back, ending up to windward of you. Stay far enough away from the mark as you approach it so you can round it properly. If a competitor is very close behind you, head up sharply after passing the mark to discourage any efforts to cut in to windward of you.

Rounding Marks

MARKS SHOULD BE ROUNDED SO THAT THE SHORTEST TOTAL DISTANCE IS traveled in the process. This means staying far enough above the mark when approaching it so that when you actually pass the mark, you have made half of your turn to the course you will follow after rounding the mark. A customary error is in just clearing the mark when approaching it, then swinging wide away from it in the process of rounding it.

The sloppiest job of rounding a mark is usually done when it is necessary to jibe at the mark. A much larger radius should be allowed for in approaching a mark where a jibe is necessary than when approaching a mark at which any other operation is to be performed. When you must jibe a mark, the only time you should approach it closely is when there is a high wind and you are on the verge of jibing when you approach the mark. In this case it is wise to come close to the mark on the approach and not jibe until even with the mark, as the wind and the boat may take charge immediately after the jibe; and if you have stayed away from the mark on the approach and jibed as you are still approaching the mark, you may easily lose control of the situation and either hit the mark or not be able to round it. This is particularly true if you are planing as you approach the mark.

On a beat with high winds and big waves, do not try to cut too close to the marks. A wave may either throw you over onto the mark; or, if the mark is a light buoy or a rowboat, it may toss it over onto you. Also, a puff may heel you over so that your sail touches the top of the flagpole, even if your hull is clearing by a good margin. This same advice applies also with a very light shifty wind, as a sudden drop in the wind may make you drift onto the mark; and particularly if there are other boats around restricting your maneuvering, a sudden shift may put you onto the mark. In any case, always try to round the windward mark from a starboard tack. Even when you think you have a clear approach to a mark on a port tack, starboard tackers seem to show up in droves out of nowhere to pick you off.

Usually even more fouls occur at marks than at the start. Everyone of course wants to get around the mark first, and things happen so fast that unless the skippers know the rules well enough to apply them without stopping to think, fouls are likely to result. The rules are quite clear in most respects, but it takes a lot of studying to know in a split second just how they apply. If you aren't sure, stay out of the mess and look up the rule when you get home. The next time you will know it.

Basically, if your boat is overlapped on the inside of the boat ahead, you have right of way and the boat ahead must give you room to round the mark. The overlap is determined when the lead boat comes within two of her overall lengths of the mark. If you have an overlap at that point, the lead boat must give you room, even if you subsequently lose the overlap. The mark is not usually an obstruction so you cannot hail a boat to tack. The easiest way to remember your rights at the windward mark is to decide what the situation would be if the mark was not there (Figure 28).

At the mark terminating a downwind leg a starboard-tack boat must give a port-tack boat room if the port tacker has an overlap. Room here includes enough space to permit the inside boat to tack or jibe if it is necessary. If you touch a mark you must re-round the mark or protest, even if the boat that caused you to hit the mark retires or accepts an alternate penalty. If you touch a mark on the side opposite the side to be rounded, then you have to round the mark first, then re-round it (Figure 29).

When the course is laid out so that marks are left to starboard, the starboard tack loses some of its advantages at the windward mark (Figure 30) if the port-tack skipper is smart enough. These situations will arise frequently on starboard courses, and are worth studying carefully.

It is never a good idea to try to lay the mark on a few long tacks, particularly if the wind is shifty. It is always better to save a short tack to use close to the mark. It is surprising how often you will find that you would have overstood the mark if you had not tacked earlier, saving another tack to use close to the mark. One exception to this advice occurs if you are being covered approaching a mark

HAILING RIGHTS AT MARKS RANKING AS OBSTRUCTIONS

A cannot fetch mark which ranks as an obstruction, being a craft at anchor, but safe piloting does not require B to do anything even though A must tack to fetch mark, so B cannot hail A about. B can probably tack closely enough behind A so A cannot tack in front of her.

A can fetch mark, so B cannot hail A about. Neither B nor C can fetch mark, but C cannot hail B about because of presence of A, even if safe piloting had required C to take action. Here as above, C can probably force B to go beyond the mark before tacking.

Neither A nor B can fetch mark, which ranks as an obstruction as it is a craft at anchor; but safe piloting does not require action by B, so B cannot hail A about.

FIGURE 28

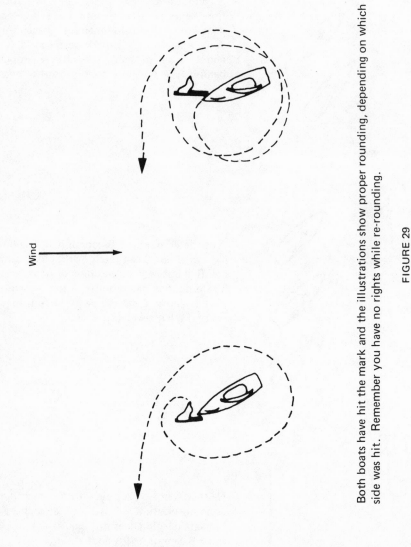

Both boats have hit the mark and the illustrations show proper rounding, depending on which side was hit. Remember you have no rights while re-rounding.

FIGURE 29

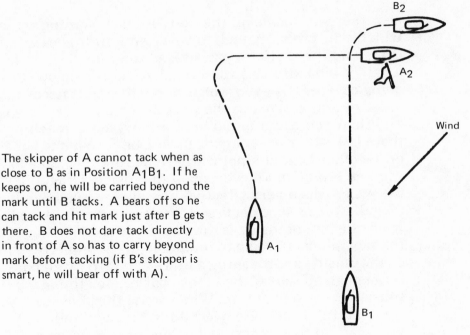

The skipper of A cannot tack when as
close to B as in Position A₁B₁. If he
keeps on, he will be carried beyond the
mark until B tacks. A bears off so he
can tack and hit mark just after B gets
there. B does not dare tack directly
in front of A so has to carry beyond
mark before tacking (if B's skipper is
smart, he will bear off with A).

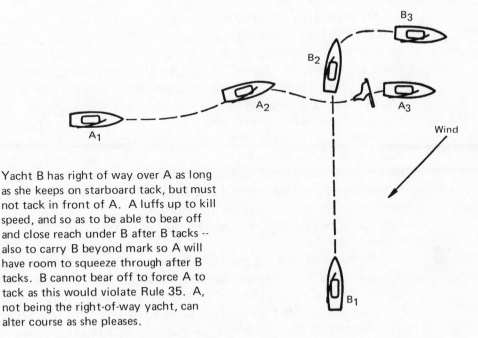

Yacht B has right of way over A as long
as she keeps on starboard tack, but must
not tack in front of A. A luffs up to kill
speed, and so as to be able to bear off
and close reach under B after B tacks --
also to carry B beyond mark so A will
have room to squeeze through after B
tacks. B cannot bear off to force A to
tack as this would violate Rule 35. A,
not being the right-of-way yacht, can
alter course as she pleases.

FIGURE 30

or if there are boats on the opposite tack coming up to the mark which will probably tack to cover you. In this case it is better to overstand the mark on purpose, as you may find yourself making a half dozen extra tacks as a result of falling below the mark from being covered. Or even worse, you will find it necessary to jibe in order to find a place in the parade. This can be very costly.

When you are approaching a mark on a reach or a run and there is another boat outside of you, be sure not to get clear ahead of the other boat at a point where he might be able to cut behind you and establish an overlap on the inside. Dragging your foot in the water was a very effective way of slowing down but it is now illegal. Also, be sure not to sail up close to the mark and then swing wide after rounding it, as the outside boat can then cut inside you. Insist on plenty of room to round the mark properly. When you are on the outside approaching a mark and fairly well back, swing out far enough so that if the other boat rounds the mark improperly you can cut inside of him. When doing this, however, you must be very careful as you are overtaking him to windward, and unless you head up just as fast as he does after rounding the mark you will be disqualified. Also, don't hit either the other boat or the mark as you have no right of way. You are taking a calculated risk and had better be sure you can make it before you go barging in.

Note that in tacking or jibing around a mark, luffing rights are determined by the relative positions of the two boats when the tack or jibe is completed. If the skipper of the windward boat is even with or ahead of the mast of the leeward boat, when the jibe or tack is completed, the leeward boat may not luff above its normal course. In this case, it is a good idea for the skipper of the windward boat to yell "mast abeam" to prevent any arguments.

However, luffing rights do not change merely because a mark has been rounded—that is, luffing rights do not change between two boats rounding a mark off a reach or run when they stay overlapped on the same tack and merely head up on a beat. Several examples are given in Figures 31, 32, 33, and 34 of when luffing rights do and do not change at marks, and how they change when they do.

When rounding a mark off a reach or a run and going onto a beat to windward on the same tack, the sails must be trimmed and the boat headed on the correct course immediately. Any time lost sagging off below the correct course or even on the correct course with the sails flapping will almost certainly let a close competitor work upwind of you. An experienced crew can help greatly in this maneuver. Trimming the main requires pulling in more feet of sheet than the jib so the jib should be either trimmed in first and

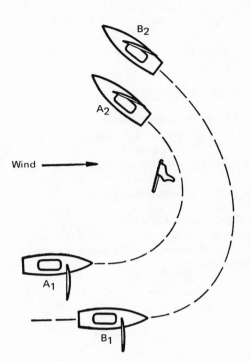

When A and B round the mark without tacking
and are overlapped all during the rounding of
the mark, luffing rights do not change merely
because the mark has been rounded. If B
could luff A before rounding, she can still do
so until the skipper of A is abeam of the mast
of B. If B could not luff A before rounding
the mark, she cannot do so after rounding as
long as the same overlap exists.

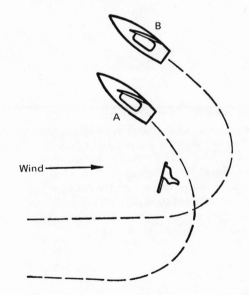

In this case, both A and B have rounded a
mark without tacking; however, A has been
clear astern of B in the process of cutting
inside of B and, therefore, a new overlap
exists. B can now luff A until the skipper
of A is abeam of the mast of B.

FIGURE 31

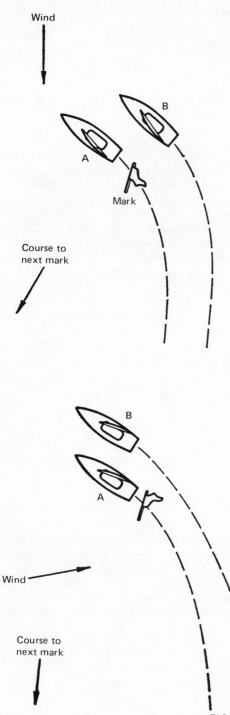

Wind

B

A

Mark

Course to
next mark

If A has luffing rights over B at the time
the mark is reached, A can carry B beyond
the mark if desired. However, if A does not
have luffing rights for any reason (the
skipper of B has at one time during the
existence of the overlap been abeam of
the mast of A or was ahead of the mast of
A when the overlap was established), A
must immediately upon rounding the mark
head on her normal course, which is for the
next mark.

B

A

Wind

Course to
next mark

There is no circumstance under which B can
force A to tack here. If B has luffing rights,
she can luff A as she pleases, but cannot
force A to tack. If B does not have luffing
rights, she can still probably luff A as her
normal course is actually on the opposite
tack. A must not touch B under any
circumstances, but there is no rule requiring
A to tack to her normal course.

FIGURE 32

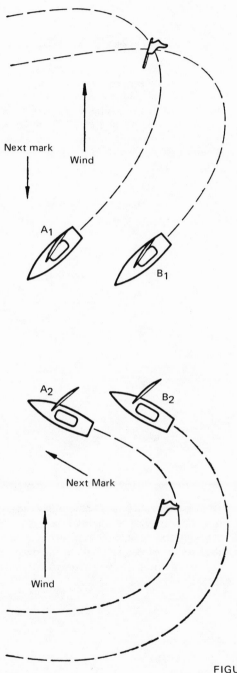

At 1, B has rounded the mark sloppily and has tacked to port tack. A has rounded the mark close and has also tacked to port. When A completes her tack, the skipper of B is behind the mast of A, a new overlap has been established, and A has luffing rights.

At 2, both yachts have jibed. When the jibe was completed, the skipper of A was ahead of the mast of B so B cannot luff.

FIGURE 33

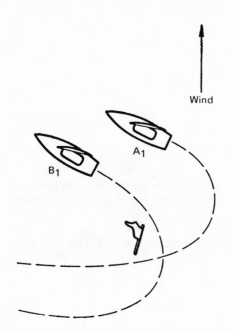

Wind

At 1, both yachts have jibed, with B cutting inside. In this case, A held too close to the mark before jibing, and at the completion of the jibe, the skipper of B was ahead of the mast of A, so A cannot luff B.

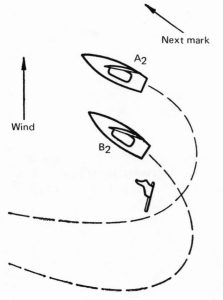

Next mark

Wind

At 2, both yachts have jibed with A again holding too close to the mark before jibing. B swung too wide and cut inside of A, but the skipper of B is still behind the mast of A when the jibe is completed, so A can luff B.

FIGURE 34

cleated by the crew who then trims the main, or better yet the crew trims the jib partially then hands the sheet to the skipper who can trim it fast enough to keep it full with one hand while the crew has both hands to trim the main. In case a jibe is necessary at the mark (if you could have jibed before getting to the mark you should have) the crew should pull the jib over and cleat it at about a broad reach position before the main is jibed. The exchange of sheets should take place just before the main jibes.

After rounding the mark, head up closer into the wind than you think is necessary, even to the point of letting the jib luff for a moment. You should have a little extra speed left over from the reach which you can use to work to windward, and this will also discourage anyone who has tried to cut between you and the mark.

When you are on the outside approaching the mark and you are too far up on the other boat to make it practical to swing out and then try to cut inside, stay as close to the inside boat as you safely can until you have rounded the mark. If you see that you will be far enough up to get a safe leeward position, work up to windward all you can without sailing above your normal course and do your best for the safe leeward position (Figure 35). However, if you see, as you round the mark, that you will not be able to get a safe leeward position after rounding it, start bearing off a little when you are halfway around the mark. Keep your sheets a little slack as you continue to bear off and try to run through the wind shadow of the windward boat (Figure 36).

When rounding a mark off a reach when the next leg is a beat to windward on the opposite tack, it is a good idea to harden up and hold the boat close-hauled on the same tack for a few seconds in order to get a little way away from the mark. If an attempt is made to flop around from a reach onto a beat on the opposite tack, particularly if there are any waves and you have a light boat, it is likely to stop and hit the mark. With large heavy boats this will not be necessary.

When rounding a mark off a reach or a run, remember that the question of an overlap depends on the position of the bow of the following boat in relation to a line through the transom of the leading boat and perpendicular to the centerline of the leading boat as the lead boat reaches the two-boat length circle. If you are the lead boat and there is no overlap, you should hail "No Overlap—No Room." You should not alter course towards the mark until you reach the circle, as this might give the following boat an overlap that she would not otherwise have. (See Figure 37.) If you are the following boat and you have an overlap, you should hail for room at the mark. The rules do not re-

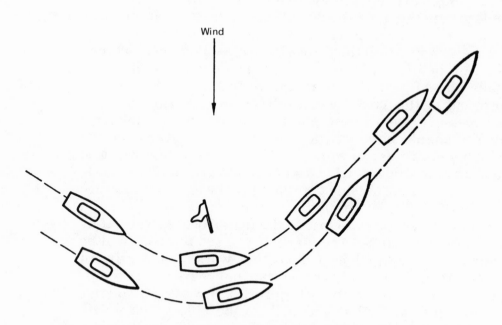

Getting a safe leeward position on a beat after rounding a mark from a reach.
Leeward boat must not head above normal course unless it had luffing rights
before rounding mark. The bow of the leeward boat must stay ahead of the
bow of the windward boat all the time during the rounding of the mark for
this maneuver to be successful, and the leeward one must stay as close as
possible to the windward one.

FIGURE 35

Wind

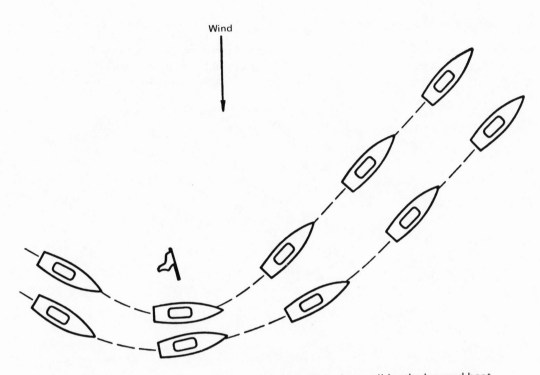

When it is apparent that a safe leeward position will be impossible, the leeward boat bears off just enough to keep its wind clear. If it is faster than the windward boat, it will gradually draw ahead and then, by pinching a trifle, can backwind the windward boat. The pinching must not be started until the leeward boat is clear ahead of the windward one or it will not be successful.

FIGURE 36

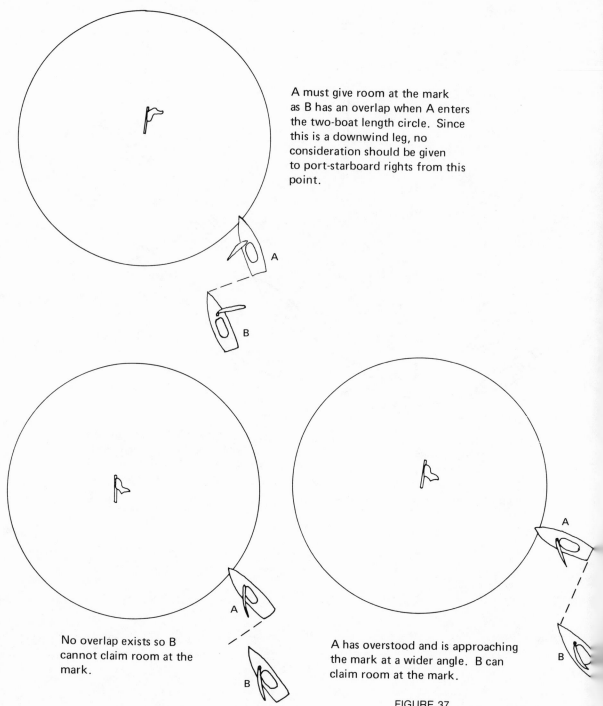

A must give room at the mark as B has an overlap when A enters the two-boat length circle. Since this is a downwind leg, no consideration should be given to port-starboard rights from this point.

No overlap exists so B cannot claim room at the mark.

A has overstood and is approaching the mark at a wider angle. B can claim room at the mark.

FIGURE 37

quire hailing but it certainly helps to support the claim.

Some skippers get confused by the rule giving room to a yacht having an overlap and try to extend that to permitting tacking at the mark when they please. The rules on tacking and jibing close aboard another yacht are entirely separate from the rule on sea room and apply at marks as well as anywhere else. See Figure 38.

When rounding a windward mark onto a run, with a large number of close-hauled boats approaching the mark, it is desirable to stay on a starboard tack for awhile until there are fewer close-hauled boats to tangle with. By staying on the starboard tack, only the starboard-tack, close-hauled boats will have right of way over you, which simplifies greatly your problems in getting back through the fleet. Also, give the close-hauled boats plenty of room. If the close-hauled boat just thinks he had to bear off, you may have trouble proving that he didn't if you cut it close. Theoretically, the boat running free might be considered the leeward boat if the close-hauled boat would just barely touch the transom of the boat running free. I don't believe this would be upheld on a protest, however.

When rounding a mark onto a run and the jib after rounding the mark onto the run will be on the same side as it is before rounding, some time can be saved by clipping the pole onto the jib sheet before rounding the mark and putting the pole out just as the mark is rounded. Don't try this in a high wind or if there is any doubt about whether the next leg is a close or broad reach.

When you are approaching a windward mark that you can almost, but not quite lay, you can frequently "shoot" it. This is merely heading the boat to windward and letting the forward motion of the boat carry it up to the mark and around. The important point is to keep full speed on the boat and at the right time, head up and around. The heavier the boat the more momentum it will have. It rarely pays to shoot a mark when you are much more than half a length below the lay line. It almost never pays with an adverse current or when the wind is very light or if there is much chop.

When rounding the windward mark with enough wind so planing conditions exist, don't yield to the temptation to relax as you round the mark. Stay hiked out, slack the sheets and pump them, and you may pop right up on a plane. You can take care of the barber hauler, centerboard, clew outhaul, Cunningham rig, and mast puller later.

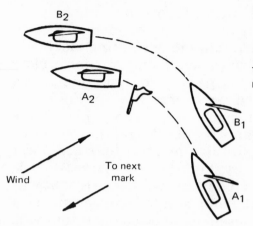

B must give A room at the mark, and cannot tack after rounding the mark until A has rounded and has tacked.

A cannot tack in front of B. A must wait until B has tacked before doing so herself.

B cannot claim room to tack at the mark, Yacht A being on the starboard tack has the right of way.

FIGURE 38

6

Sailing on the Free Legs of the Course

WHEN REACHING AND PRESSED BY OTHER BOATS CLOSE BEHIND, IT IS DIF-
ficult to choose the best tactics. In general, it is best to stay directly
ahead of the boat immediately behind you, particularly if he is
your most dangerous competitor. However, if there is still another
boat close behind and he is smart, he will bear off to get clear wind
and is very likely to get to the next mark first or at least on the
inside with an overlap if you head very far upwind. If you bear off
and try to stay in front of him, the boat immediately behind you
is likely to harden up on the wind and be able to shoot up just
enough to blanket you. If it is a fairly close reach and the wind may
shift against you, it is best to stay pretty well to windward. Falling
below the mark and having to tack for it will be fatal.

When covering on a reach or a run, remember that the region
in which you are taking another boat's wind extends about three
mast lengths to leeward in the direction of the *apparent* wind.
This looks complicated on paper, but on the water it is simple—
your wind pennant is pointing in the direction of your wind
shadow (Figure 39).

The best thing to do is to decide who is the most dangerous
competitor in the end and try to stay ahead of him. In any case, do
not get enticed into a luffing match. The only person who wins in
a luffing match is the third man back who did not get into the
match, except in very rare circumstances.

Since luffing is costly for everyone, the secret is to avoid it. If
you find a boat coming up to windward on you, a good sharp luff
before an overlap occurs will usually discourage the following

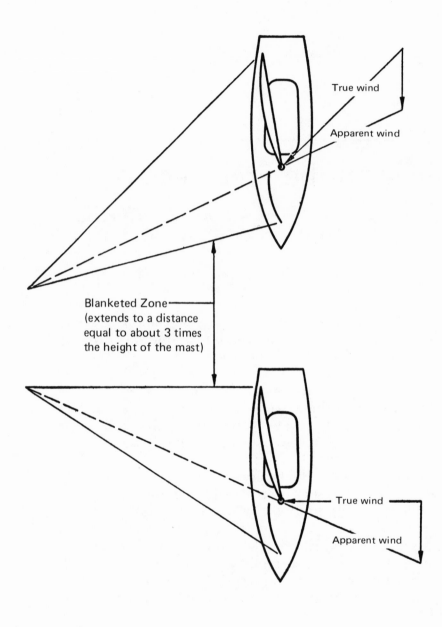

True wind

Apparent wind

Blanketed Zone
(extends to a distance
equal to about 3 times
the height of the mast)

True wind

Apparent wind

FIGURE 39

boat, and he will go off to leeward of you. If it is a faster boat, it will probably take you anyway, so it is better to bear off and let him go on by—it is better to lose one boat than half the fleet if you take a wide detour. By the same token, if you are being luffed and can't quite get mast abeam, it is better to break out of the luffing match and bear off. Letting the sails flap momentarily will slow you down enough to permit you to go to leeward.

There are still a great many skippers who do not know the rules on luffing as well as they should, even when marks aren't involved. Since a lack of this knowledge may get you into trouble, and easily, Figures 40 through 44 should be carefully studied.

If you are behind and on a broad reach or a run, you can very often pick up several boats by bearing off several hundred feet below the others so your wind is clear, and while the others are chasing each other—and you hope engaging in luffing matches—you will be able to sail the shortest course to the next mark and may catch them. This is an especially good maneuver if bearing off will put you on the inside of the next mark. It may not be so good if it puts you on the outside on a short course. If you know your boat is fast off the wind, it is always a good gamble even if you have to go a longer distance to get clear wind, and if you are sure the wind can't shift enough to make you tack to make the mark when you get there. If it is a fairly close reach and if the wind has been at all shifty, it will be better to try to pass to windward.

In trying this stunt of bearing off to go to leeward of other boats, don't forget that if an overtaking yacht is steering a course to pass to leeward and is clearly within three overall lengths, the leading yacht shall not sail below her normal course. What this means is that if you are going to bear off on the free leg of the course, do so immediately on rounding the windward mark, and do a good thorough job of bearing off to discourage the boat behind you from doing the same thing. If he rounds the mark within three overall lengths of you and steers a course to go to leeward of you, you are sunk—you must hold your normal course until he gets clear ahead or gives up and heads to windward of you, or you get more than three lengths ahead of him.

When behind on a reach that is broad enough so that the boats have their whisker poles out, and where it does not appear desirable to bear off to get clear wind because of being close to the next mark and bearing off will put you on the outside at the mark, you can frequently catch the boat ahead of you by gradually working upwind until only a few degrees from the point where the jib will not draw well. Inform your crew that as soon as he sees the tiller move he is to get the pole in and trim the sheets on the opposite

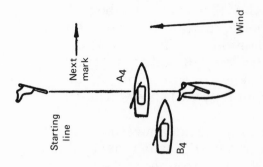

This example commences before the starting gun. At Position 1, A is clear astern of B, overtaking B. At Position 2, A has overtaken B to leeward and may luff B gradually but not above a close-hauled course. At position 3, B is well behind the mast abeam position and A may luff B as far as she pleases. At position 4, A must give B room to clear the committee boat, but thereafter may luff as far and as fast as she pleases.

FIGURE 40

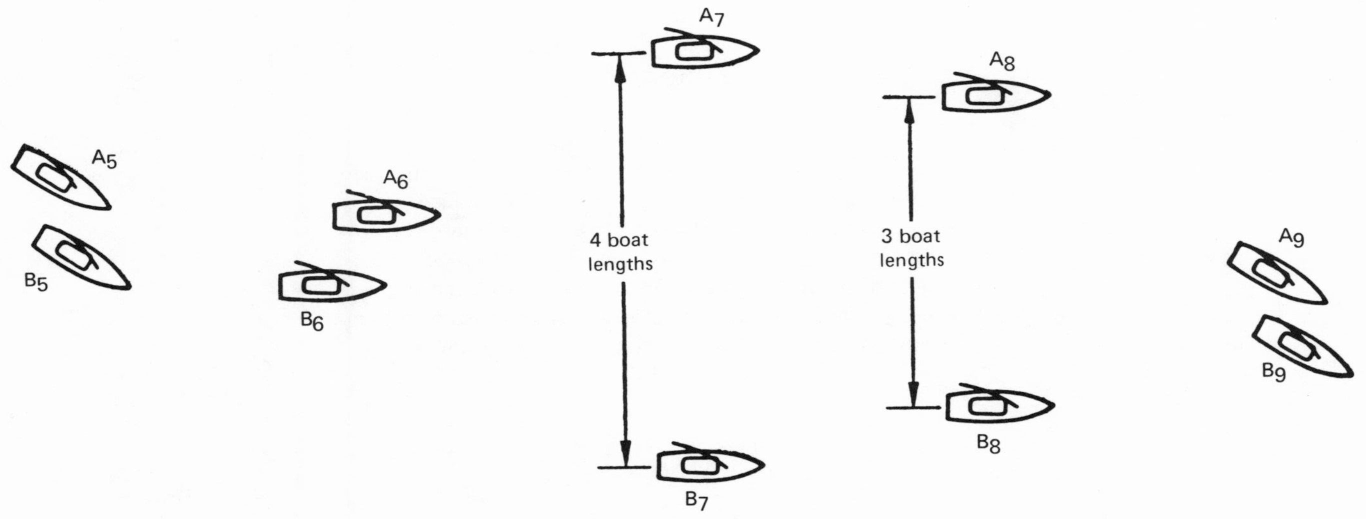

The skipper of B5 is abeam of the mast of A5 so A must resume her normal course. Even though the skipper of B6 is now behind the mast of A6, A cannot luff while this overlap exists. At 7, the overlap has terminated as the yachts are more than three overall lengths apart. At 8, a new overlap is established. Since the skipper of B is behind the mast of A, A can again luff B. At 9, A has again lost luffing rights as the skipper of B is abeam of the mast of A.

FIGURE 41

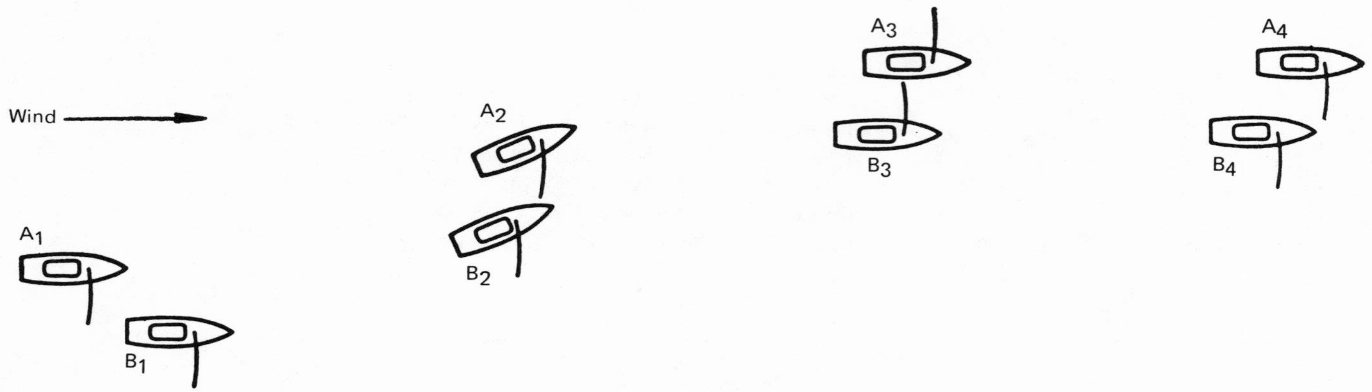

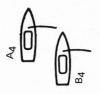

At Position A₂B₂, the skipper of A is ahead of the mast of B and B must therefore resume her normal course. At Position A₃B₃, both boats jibe. B is now the windward boat and as the skipper of B is behind the mast of A, A can luff B. At A₄B₄, both yachts have jibed again. This time the skipper of A is ahead of the mast of B at the time the jibe is completed, and therefore, B cannot luff A.

FIGURE 42

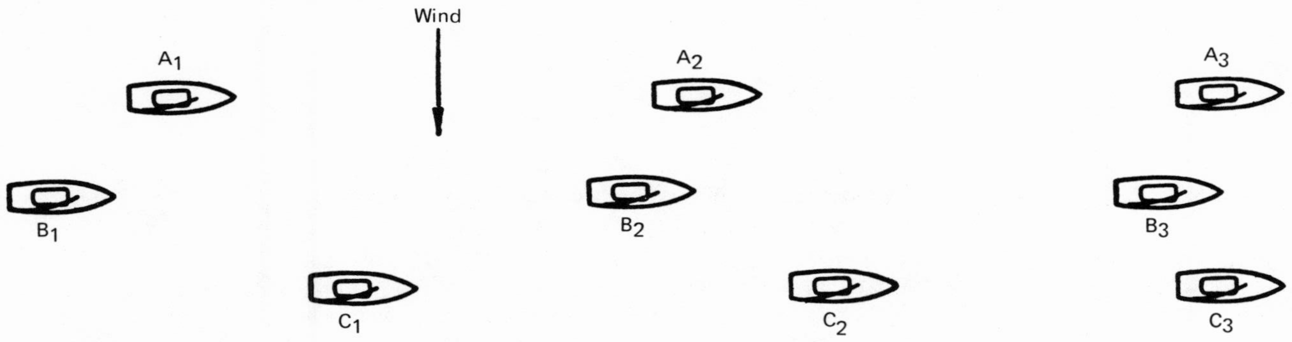

At $A_1B_1C_1$, no overlap exists. At $A_2B_2C_2$, B has overtaken A to leeward and cannot luff A. At $A_3B_3C_3$, A and B have overtaken C to windward. C has luffing rights over both A and B, and A must respond to a luff by B and C, even though B does not have luffing rights over A.

FIGURE 43

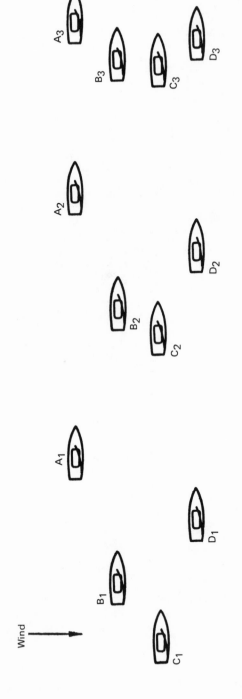

At $A_1B_1C_1D_1$, no overlap exists. At $A_2B_2C_2D_2$, C has overtaken B and both are about to overtake D. At $A_3B_3C_3D_3$, B and C have overtaken D to windward which would give D luffing rights over both B and C. However, all three yachts have overtaken A to leeward and none of them have luffing rights on A. D may luff B and C only until they would interfere with A.

FIGURE 44

side without your saying anything. Then when you are quite close to the boat ahead, and at a moment when he is not watching you, head up sharply. The chances are that he will try to luff you and in the process his jib will collapse and the crew, not being warned, will bungle the job of getting the pole in. Then you have him.

If there is a mob of boats closely bunched approaching a mark on a broad reach or a run, it is better to be inside and behind than well up front and outside. This is particularly important as the inside position is the windward position after rounding the mark and boats which were well behind you but inside may end up ahead of you after rounding the mark. If you see that this is likely to happen, the best thing to do is to drop back and cut through the mob of boats, going behind as many as necessary, but in any case get on the inside before you reach the mark.

When trying to catch another boat on a run, blanketing is effective only when you are fairly close, and the wake of the boat ahead is quite effective in slowing down the following boat. In a light wind you can frequently catch a leading boat better by staying out of his wake and not trying to blanket him, at least until you are very close to him. In a high wind, particularly if planing is possible, blanketing is more effective and the wake is less effective. Once in awhile, in a good strong breeze, a slower boat can get a free ride behind a faster one which has just passed the slow one by getting on the stern wave of the leading boat and coasting down it. This works particularly well if a larger but not too much faster class is racing at the same time and you can hook a ride behind one of them.

When approaching a mark or the finish line, do not try to blanket another boat when too far away from the mark or finish line. If you blanket him too early, you may get clear ahead of him and then he will go to work on you. Do not wait so long that you will have an argument as to whether your overlap at a mark was established in time, but also do not start so early that you draw clear ahead and are in turn blanketed.

When running before the wind in shifty winds, particularly if they are light, jibe as often as necessary, as a good jibe can be done without losing any speed. A latch fitting on the end of the whisker pole which holds the pole to the jib sheet is essential to efficient jibing. The crew should pull the pole back and put it out on the other side while the skipper handles the jib sheets. In a light wind the crew can do this with one hand and throw the boom over with the other hand. Jibing with a spinnaker can be done just about as fast, if you have proper equipment. Release the forward guy after the sheet has been slacked, if necessary, so that the end of the pole can be reached. In the meantime the skipper heads the boat slowly out of the wind. The pole is then removed from the fitting on the mast, the forward guy is attached to it (if you have provision to do this), and the pole is then attached to the former clew of the spinnaker which now becomes the tack. The opposite end of the pole is released from the former tack of the spinnaker, and as the boom swings over, the pole is attached to the mast, the sheets are trimmed, and practically no speed has been lost.

Some authorities recommend tacking when going downwind, so that the boat is never running directly before the wind. Admittedly, the position directly before the wind is the slowest point of sailing—but a straight line is still the shortest distance between two points. It is my opinion that ordinarily nothing is gained by tacking downwind, but also that within limits nothing will be lost either. If the wind velocity is marginal for planing and you can get the boat to plane by heading up a little from the course dead before the wind, it will really pay to go fairly far off course. If you can plane just as well directly before the wind, it won't pay. Tacking downwind and with an appreciable tide is another story, which will be covered later.

If you have never done much race committee work race watching, you will be surprised at how far off course the pack will deviate to windward on reaches. Everyone is trying to maintain clear air and so heads up to keep following boats from driving over him. A good technique to gain a few boats is to deviate to leeward just after you round the mark. It must be done emphatically to let the following boats know you are not going to join the pack. After heading off to leeward for several boat lengths, set your course directly for the next mark. It will appear that all the boats to windward are passing you, but they are going way off course and what goes up must come down. Meanwhile, you have relatively clear air and no interference. Nine times out of ten you will pick up boats.

On a reach there are two times when following the shortest distance won't make the shortest time. These are when the wind is very puffy and either quite light or quite heavy. Under these conditions, it pays to head fairly far upwind during the lulls and bear off on the puffs. In a light puffy wind, this enables you to get the puffs sooner and ride them longer. In a wind that is just high enough for planing, you can plane with less wind while heading up, and then when the puff comes along, you can continue planing while bearing off and getting back to your normal course.

When running before the wind, remember that the starboard tack always has right of way. If you are on a port tack and are being overtaken by a boat on starboard tack, even though he is on your windward side, he has the right of way. You must either jibe over to a starboard tack yourself, or else figure out how to keep clear of him by some other means (unless you are about to round the leeward mark, in which case the starboard-tack boat loses its right of way).

7

Drifting Matches

A RACE WHEN THE WIND VARIES FROM NOTHING AT ALL TO VERY LITTLE more and shifts all over the compass is very appropriately known as a drifting match. About the only good advice I can give to one facing a drifting match is to give up sailing and take up outboard motor racing. The only thing you can be sure of is that 90 percent of what you do will seem to be wrong, unless you are in the lead. Then it will be 100 percent. Sometimes local knowledge helps, but even that backfires about as often as it works.

If you are on a beat, tack with every shift so as to always be on the tack heading closest to the mark, but if you see a better-than-average puff get into it as soon as possible even if you will not be on the tack heading closest to the mark. Sometimes the puffs travel along the water, and if you see ripples on the water in the direction from which the wind is coming, you can count on it getting to you. Other times, however, the wind seems to go straight up in the air after reaching a certain line and never moves across the water. If the puff is the type that moves and you are on a beat, you will get it about as soon on one tack as on the other. However, if the puff seems to be the stationary variety and it isn't too far away it will pay you to tack and go for it—or to bear off and reach for it if it looks like a good one, but doesn't seem to be moving.

Shore lines are particularly tricky during drifting matches. Generally they are dangerous, but you still have to watch them carefully as once in a great while a breeze will come along close to a shore and never get far away from the shore. When sailing against a strong tide in a drifting match, the decision on how close to go to a shore becomes especially important. If the ripples on the water indicate that the breeze is about as good close to shore, it will pay to get there as fast as possible, tacking away from the mark or bearing off from a beat to a reach as the case may be, in order to get into the slower tide as quickly as possible. If this condition exists before the start of the race, it should be the deciding factor in making your start. If your speed through the water is practically nothing, it will pay to completely ignore your normal course for a long enough time to get over to where the tide is less if you can then go in the general direction of the mark.

On a reach in a drifting match, it is a good idea to stay well upwind. Bearing off to try to pass a bunch of boats is quite hazardous, as the boats to windward get the puffs first and can ride them longer, and the puffs frequently seem to fizzle out before they get very far down to leeward. Reaching along a shore line with an off-shore breeze presents a nice problem in trying to decide how far upwind and therefore how close to the shore to go. The windward boats of course get the puffs first, but the wind is usually stronger a little farther out from shore, particularly if the shore is high. About all you can do is experiment and watch other boats. Heading up between puffs and bearing off with them will pay big dividends under these circumstances.

A run directly before the wind is likely to be the most heartbreaking part of a drifting match for the leaders as everything favors the boats behind. They very frequently pick up a puff and then when the puff dies, coast on their momentum right up on the leaders. This generally results in the boats being fairly closely bunched towards the end of at least the first downwind leg. When this happens there is a stunt which, if everything works right, will frequently let you catch a pack of boats that are a little ahead of you. This is to watch behind you and when you see a puff coming, reach past the sterns of several other boats until you have built up the maximum speed you can get, then head downwind again. If you timed everything right and if the puff was a little one, as they generally are in drifting matches, the speed which you built up by reaching before the wind got to them will carry you on past them by the time the puff dies. Save this stunt until fairly close to the mark when it will be too late for someone else to try it on you.

The main thing is not to worry if you are behind—you are probably better off than if you were leading—and do not start jumping around doing silly things just because nothing seems to be happening. Winning a drifting match is 95 percent luck—all you can do is to make the most of that other 5 percent.

The most important thing to *not* do if you are in the lead seems to be to try to cover the fleet by taking a middle course. There is no scientific reason that I can find for this, but on a number of occasions I have been well in the lead when the wind dropped. To play it safe, I thought, I would hold a middle course—and I have had boats sail around me on both sides. The only possible reason that I can think of for this is that when you are in the middle, you have a tendency to dash off in all directions and to be constantly trying to use someone else's worn-out wind instead of finding your own. There is a tendency, which is fatal, to watch other boats and try to get over near them just because they have a momentary puff. By the time you get near them that puff is gone, and before another one comes along there, there probably has been one back where you were.

If you happen to get a poor start and the first leg is a beat, it will not pay to tack purely for the sake of getting clear. The leaders can detect wind shifts much better than you can, and if you split tacks the chances are you are sailing off on a poorer tack than they are on. Also, it takes so long to get about with no wind and takes so long to get started again that each unnecessary tack is terribly costly. The best thing to do is just to tack with the leaders until the boats get spread out more, then go on your own if you think you can outsmart them. If they cover you, just relax and wait until later to get them.

In a drifting match be very cautious when on port tack, trying to cross in front of a starboard tacker. He may catch a little puff you don't get and catch you helpless. Also, if you decide to tack in front of or under another boat, be sure you have about four times as much room as you think you need. A puff of wind or a shift may alter your relative positions suddenly.

Many sailors do not work as hard in drifters as they should. It is boring and frustrating, and nearly everyone hates them with a passion. But drifters require a great deal of concentration, probably more than in any other conditions. The lighter the wind, the more apt it is to be shifty, and if you don't concentrate, you will miss shifts and slight gusts. Done properly, a drifter is physically exhausting.

In order to get the maximum boat speed, sails must be sheeted very loosely, especially the mainsail since with little or no wind, the leech will hook badly if trimmed too tightly. The front part of the sail may be luffing (although you won't be able to see it), but at least the aft part is not presenting a broadside surface to the wind. Keep the boat heeled about 20 degrees to leeward so gravity will help the sails hold their shape. Above all, keep the boat as still as possible—movement tends to shake your sails and stall your boat. In order to adjust yourself to the conditions, conversation should be kept to a minimum and what conversation is necessary should be done in whispers. Don't make abrupt movements and talk loud—it will wake the baby!

Tell tales are not much help in drifters, and about the only way to find out what the wind is doing is to use cigarette or punk smoke. Tacking as well as tiller movement will slow you down, so try adjusting your sails to the conditions rather than changing direction of the boat. Much more sail adjustment is needed in drifters. If you do tack, make a good roll-tack with a couple of strong pushes on the tiller. In an almost flat calm drifter, roll-tacking may not work. The lighter the boat is, the better chance you have. I would guess that if you try more than one roll per come about, you could be protested for "rocking" which is not legal under any circumstances. If one roll and a couple of shoves on the tiller will get you around, you are probably all right if you can justify the tack. Frequent successful roll-tacks without pretty obvious justification from wind shifts which have caused everybody to tack are likely to be considered the equivalent of "pumping." Every four years as the racing rules are changed this rule is especially susceptible to change. Keep up to date on the rules and appeal decisions.

8

Tides and River Currents

STRICTLY SPEAKING, THE TIDE IS THE PERIODIC RISE AND FALL OF WATER along the coast caused by the attraction of the sun and moon. The tide rises for about six hours, remains stationary for a short time, then begins to recede and falls for about six hours. The rise is the flood tide, and the fall is the ebb tide. The term "high water" is used at the peak of the flood tide, and "low water" is used at the lowest point of the ebb tide. The interval between two successive periods of high or low waters is approximately 12 hours and 26 minutes, which means that the time of high or low water is about 52 minutes later each day.

Twice a month, at the new and full moons, the attraction of the moon and sun is combined, and the highest tides will occur, which are called "spring" tides. Near the first and fourth quarters of the moon, the attraction of the moon and sun are at right angles to each other, and the tide is at its lowest. This is called the "neap" tide. The height of the tide varies greatly at different points along the coast. At the Bay of Fundy and similar points where the coast contains inlets which narrow toward their head, the tide is very high. A promontory such as the Florida peninsula tends to lower the tide. Also, tides do not occur at all places on the same meridian at the same time.

The rise and fall of the tide causes currents to flow into harbors, bays, sounds, and inlets when the tide is flooding and causes these currents to flow out when the tide ebbs. The amount of current depends on the amount of water that has to get through a given channel in the time available. Therefore, the velocity of the current flowing into a small harbor through a wide entrance will be much lower than that of a current flowing into a large harbor through a narrow entrance. A high-velocity current can be felt for some distance from the inlet.

The term tide is generally used interchangeably for the true meaning of the rise and fall of the water level, and a meaning synonymous with current, and this meaning will be used in the following discussion. Also, no specific mention will be made of river currents, as they may be handled in exactly the same way as tides.

Local knowledge is of the greatest importance when sailing where there are strong tides. There are, however, certain general principles that apply everywhere and which will be discussed here. If you understand these general principles, it will be much easier to understand what the local experts are talking about in explaining the local peculiarities of the tide.

Tide is always strongest in deep water (in the center of a channel) and is generally weakest in shallow water (along the shore, or over a reef or bar). It will be slowed up, or may even be reversed, behind a point or a breakwater, but will be stronger at the end of the point. Its direction in the vicinity of the point will be affected for an appreciable distance out away from the point (Figure 45). The tide will be less immediately in front of and immediately behind an island, and will be faster between the island and the shore, if the island is large in relation to the total width of the channel (Figure 46).

The Hydrographic Office of the Department of Commerce publishes Tidal Current Charts which are very useful in providing local information. The charts show the relative tides at different spots, and show where the tides change first. They will also show where the tides don't behave according to the theories on how they should—which sometimes happens.

The most important thing to remember when sailing in the presence of tides is that the direction in which the boat is heading and the direction in which you are moving in relation to the bottom or anything tied to it may be far different. (See Figures 47 and 48, which conveniently ignore the effects of tide on apparent wind, as that comes later.) The amount of the difference increases rapidly as the speed of the wind and the tide get closer together, and decreases as the wind becomes stronger in relation to the tide. Your course and speed relative to another boat are not affected by tide unless of course one has a stronger tide than the other.

What all this adds up to, as far as racing tactics are concerned, is that you want to be sure that the course you are heading on is

EFFECT OF BAYS, HARBORS, REEFS, AND POINTS ON TIDE
(EBB TIDE)

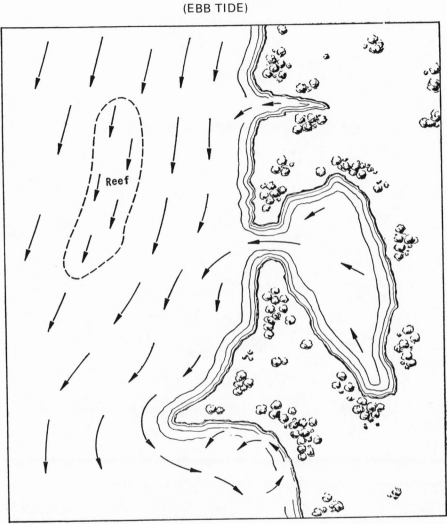

The length of the arrows is proportional to the velocity of the current which is slowest over the reef and near the shore, and fastest in the center of the channel, at the entrance to a large harbor, and at the end of a point.

FIGURE 45

EFFECT OF ISLAND ON TIDE

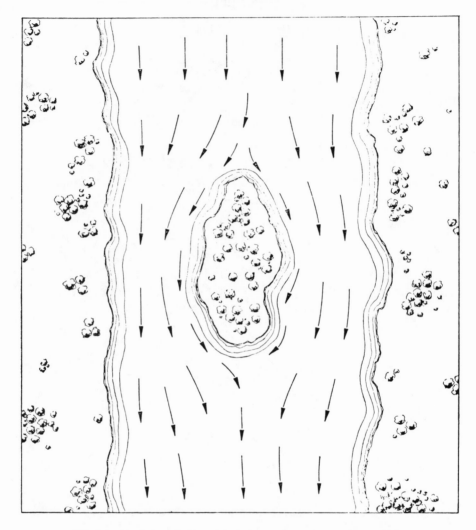

The length of the arrows again is proportional to the velocity of the current. The current is faster between the island and the shore than in the main channel because the water has less space to get through, and is slower just upstream and downstream from the island.

FIGURE 46

EFFECT OF HEAD TIDE ON COURSE SAILED
AND COURSE ACTUALLY MADE GOOD

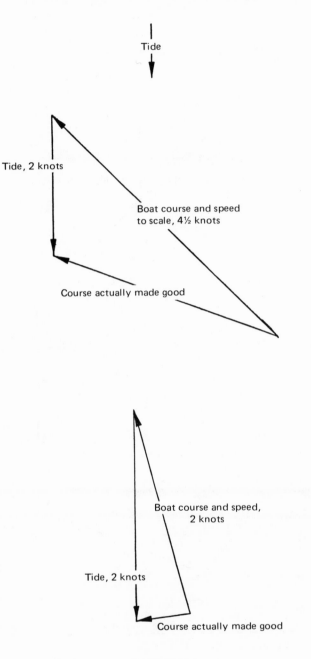

FIGURE 47

BOAT COURSE AND SPEED
AS AFFECTED BY FOLLOWING OR BEAM TIDE

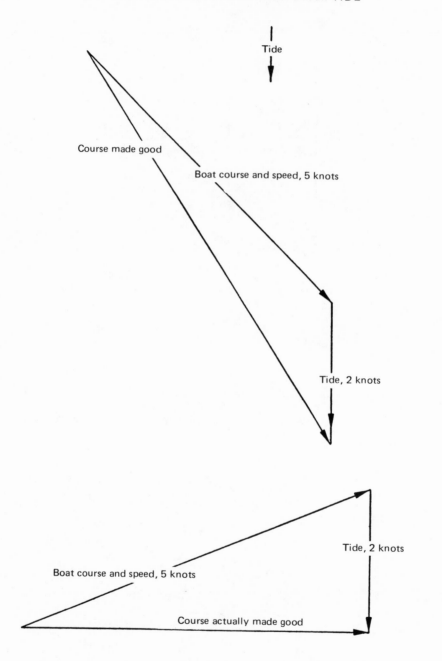

FIGURE 48

going to end you up where you want to go after taking the tide into account, and that in planning your course, you have planned it so that the tide will hinder you as little as possible when it is going against you, and help as much as possible when it is going with you. If the wind is strong and the tide weak, you can pretty much ignore it. If the wind is light and the tide strong, the tide is of paramount importance. Between these two extremes, you must decide just how much importance to assign to the tide and how much more importance you should assign to watching your competitors.

Figure 49 illustrates the smartest trick—or most foolhardy, depending on how you look at it—that was pulled off at the Snipe World's Championship at Larchmont in 1949. In one of the races, the wind was about 5 miles an hour and there was a strong head tide. The Norwegian skipper had drawn one of those boats about which nothing good could be said, but the boat captain at Larchmont Yacht Club and all the men running the tenders there were Norwegian. All of the local skippers said to stay away from Hen and Chickens Reef as you would be sure to go aground, and the reef is hard. The Norwegians either knew better or they were awfully lucky—in any case, they only took two tacks on each windward leg—one to get them onto the reef, and the other which took them the full length of it—and took first place in a boat which in the other four races took two seventh places, one eighth, and one ninth. You can't ignore the tide when the wind is light and it is strong.

When beating against a strong head tide, be sure not to point too high. The importance of this increases rapidly as the wind decreases. Your speed over the bottom then becomes a small number which is the difference between two relatively much larger numbers—the speed of the tide and your speed through the water. Suppose the tide is running against you at 2 knots, and you are making 2¼ knots through the water—leaving ¼ knot to get to the windward mark on. Now if you pinch a little and decrease your speed through the water by 10 percent, you have cut your speed toward the windward mark by almost 100 percent.

Another book on sailing recommends pinching when heading directly into a tide, on the theory that the tide will push against the side of the boat and squirt it to windward the way you can go way off to one side when you are riding on water skis behind a motor boat just by aiming your skis that way. If your sailboat were being towed by an infinitely long tow line at a steady speed this would be just fine—but when you have only sails and a wind, the theory is completely cockeyed. The tide does not affect the motion of the

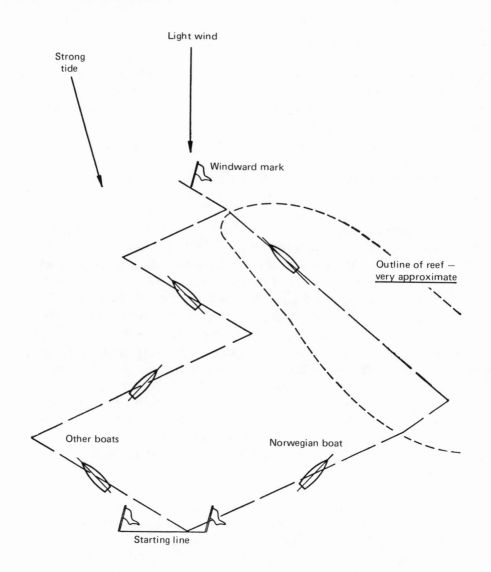

Whether they were smart or foolhardy or both may be argued, but nevertheless the Norwegians ended up way ahead in the third race of the 1949 Snipe Class World Championships at Larchmont, in a boat that never placed higher than seventh in the other races.

FIGURE 49

boat in any mysterious fashion—but it does affect the progress of the boat through the water in one way, and over the bottom in two ways. The first way in which it affects the progress of the boat over the bottom is by merely taking the boat along for the ride in the direction and at the speed at which the tide is moving, as illustrated in Figure 45. The second way in which it affects the progress of the boat over the bottom and also through the water, which becomes quite complicated if you try to calculate or illustrate its exact quantitative effect by vector diagrams is by altering the relationship between the true wind direction and velocity, and the apparent wind direction and velocity. This effect is a much exaggerated example of the one illustrated in Figure 3, page 60, which shows that a slower boat can head closer to the actual wind than a fast one.

It may be this effect that would cause a skipper who ought to know better to think he was gaining by pinching when heading directly into a head tide. What actually happens is that when heading directly into the tide, the velocity of the boat in relation to the true wind is greatly reduced, allowing the boat to head much closer to the true wind without actually pinching in relation to the apparent wind. The only thing that keeps the sails happy is having the apparent wind in the right direction—in beating against a tide in a light wind you can sail much closer to the true wind than without the tide and therefore get to windward better—but don't carry it to the point of pinching.

Figures 50 and 51 show the effect of tide on the apparent wind when beating to windward against and across the tide. The diagram illustrating beating to windward without any tide is not meant to represent the exact relationship of wind and boat speed for any specific boat, but it is representative of typical values for any small boat. The assumptions are that the most efficient course to windward is 45 degrees from the actual wind, and that a 10-knot actual wind will produce a boat speed of 4 knots. This results in the apparent wind making an angle of 32½ degrees to the centerline of the boat, which remains constant as the most efficient angle for going to windward. In the examples of beating in the presence of tide, the diagrams were made by a trial-and-error method, altering them until two requirements were met—the first, that the apparent wind must always make an angle of 32½ degrees with the boat centerline; and second, that the speed of the boat must be in proper relationship to the velocity of the apparent wind.

Figure 52 repeats two illustrations of Figures 50 and 51 showing a boat on both starboard and port tacks against and across a 2-knot tide with a 10-knot actual wind with the wind at the best

BEATING AGAINST AND WITH TIDES

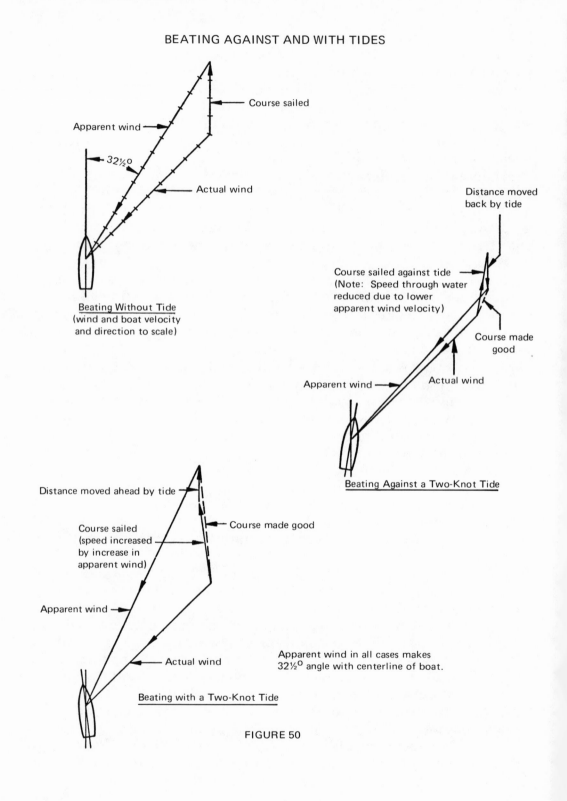

Course sailed

Apparent wind

32½°

Actual wind

Beating Without Tide
(wind and boat velocity
and direction to scale)

Distance moved
back by tide

Course sailed against tide
(Note: Speed through water
reduced due to lower
apparent wind velocity)

Course made
good

Apparent wind

Actual wind

Beating Against a Two-Knot Tide

Distance moved ahead by tide

Course sailed
(speed increased
by increase in
apparent wind)

Course made good

Apparent wind

Actual wind

Beating with a Two-Knot Tide

Apparent wind in all cases makes
32½° angle with centerline of boat.

FIGURE 50

BEATING WITH A BEAM TIDE

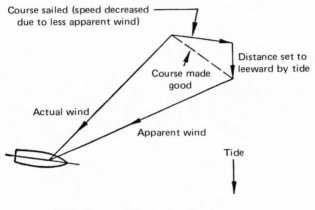

Course sailed (speed decreased due to less apparent wind)

Distance set to leeward by tide

Course made good

Actual wind

Apparent wind

Tide

Tide Setting Boat to Leeward

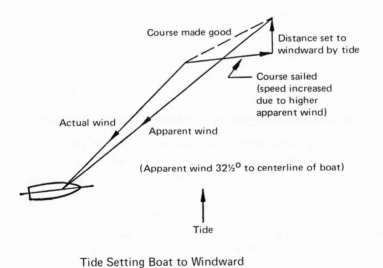

Course made good

Distance set to windward by tide

Course sailed (speed increased due to higher apparent wind)

Actual wind

Apparent wind

(Apparent wind 32½° to centerline of boat)

Tide

Tide Setting Boat to Windward

FIGURE 51

EFFECT OF PINCHING WHEN BEATING AGAINST A TIDE

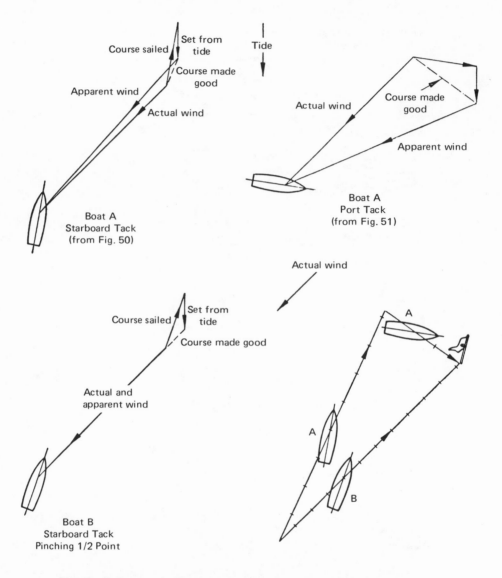

Boat B pinches one-half point when beating against tide, resulting in course made good being directly to windward. Boat A does not pinch. Since all diagrams are for the same wind and tide, the course made good for each diagram is to scale as to speed. To cover a representative distance to windward as shown, Boat B which pinches, takes 11.2 minutes, while Boat A, although traveling farther, takes 9.4 minutes.

FIGURE 52

angle. It also shows a boat pinching one-half point closer to the apparent wind than in the upper illustrations. In this case the apparent wind and the true wind are from the same direction, and the course made good is directly into the apparent wind. The boat that is pinching is certainly going to windward—but it still won't get to the mark first.

When sailing into the wind or across it with a following tide, the effect of the tide is to greatly increase the speed of the boat in relation to the true wind, thereby increasing the angle between the apparent wind and the actual wind and increasing the amount of the apparent wind. All of this is not actually as confusing as it sounds, as the skipper when racing is conscious only of the way his sails behave and of the direction of the apparent wind—he generally has no way of knowing the direction of the actual wind unless he is heading directly into it or out of it, and he really doesn't care.

When beating against a strong tide in a light wind, keep taking bearings on the shore to be sure that you are actually going somewhere in relation to the shore. When you find that you aren't—drop the anchor. If you can sneak it out without competitors seeing you, act as if you were sailing normally. They will see you suddenly start gaining on them and will start sailing frantically to go as fast as you seem to be going—and the harder they try, the faster they go backward.

Another good thing to remember when racing with a light wind and a strong tide is that the tide is obeying laws of nature and can be counted on to perform on schedule—and a light wind can't. If you are reaching in a light wind and the tide is pushing you to windward—stay well below the mark. If you get too far to windward, the wind may die and you may never get back to the mark against the tide. If you are well below the mark and the wind dies, the tide will help you get there. Conversely, if on a reach and the tide is carrying you to leeward and the wind seems at all undependable, stay well up to windward. If the wind dies, you can continue to reach for the mark, while the boats that headed directly for the mark in the first place will have a practically hopeless beat for it.

The effect of tides on starting tactics has been covered already, but might be summarized while we are talking about tides. With a head tide that is strong in relation to the wind, always hit the windward end of the line and stay very close to the line before the start. With a following tide and a light wind, hitting the leeward end is the safest; stay fairly far back of the line, and if the wind is very light, don't take any chances of being over early.

When sailing directly before the wind with a light wind and a strong following tide, tacking downwind is especially effective. The following tide has reduced the apparent wind—it may be practically nothing if the tide is strong and the wind light—and broad reaching off the wind will do a lot of good by increasing the apparent wind velocity and moving its direction so that it comes more from the beam and less from astern (Figure 53).

Local knowledge is particularly helpful when racing in a light wind at either high or slack water. The speed of the tide is of course zero at either high or slack water—but high and slack water don't always occur at the same time even over a fairly small general area. On Long Island Sound, for example, the tide starts flowing first along the shore. If you have a very light wind in which the tide will be very important, you may be able to get a boost in both directions, or at least a boost in one direction and no hindrance in the other. If it is close to slack water—and if the tide shifts first close to shore—you should stay close to the shore when heading in the direction of a flooding tide, and stay near the middle when heading in the direction of an ebb tide.

One of the things which often amazes people accustomed to making a scientific approach to the solution of problems is the frequency with which people arrive at the right answer for the wrong reason. It happens in any field connected with mechanics, science, physics, and the laws of motion—and sailing is no exception.

Obviously any skipper who is successful in racing in the presence of tides knows all the tricks about sailing in tides—but how many of them have the right answers with the wrong reasons. The main reason for this, I believe, is that very few people understand completely what tides do to the apparent wind. A complete understanding of this effect will explain the phenomena experienced sailing in the presence of tides, which are frequently ascribed to causes which just won't stand up under scientific scrutiny. Several diagrams of the effect of tide on apparent wind are given in Figures 50 and 51.

The term "lee-bowing" is used frequently in connection with sailing in the presence of tides. There seem to be several different definitions of the term, varying from the specific act of pinching when beating directly into a tide which has been mentioned earlier, to the general effect of the tide coming from the leeward side of the boat helping the boat to windward.

This effect is generally ascribed to the tide pushing against the centerboard or keel and squirting the boat to windward as if the boat were tied to something or were being towed. The statement is also frequently made that when the tide and wind are both more

RUNNING BEFORE THE WIND
WITH TIDE TACKING DOWNWIND

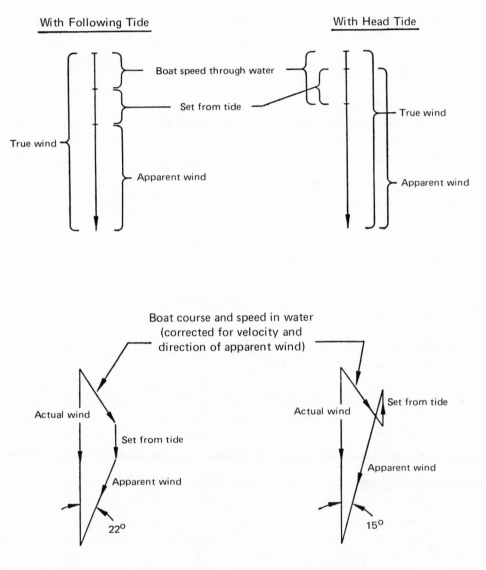

Heading out of wind by the same amount makes 50 percent more difference in direction of apparent wind with following tide as compared with head tide.

FIGURE 53

or less against the boat, the boat should head as close as possible into the tide when on a beat—which is correct. The reason given, however, is that this presents the minimum resistance to the oncoming tide, and that on the opposite tack the centerboard or keel presents a wide surface to the tide and as a result, which is of course most noticeable in a light wind and a strong tide, the boat will be set way off to leeward. The boat is set off to leeward on this tack, but not because of the width of the centerboard.

In solving any problem involving complex motions, the problem is simplified by considering the motions separately, then combining them. Let's assume that the tide and the wind are moving at the same speed and in the same direction. It is obvious under these conditions that *the boat is going to move with the tide, in relation to the bottom, in the direction of the tide and at the speed of the tide. It will go just as fast whether it is headed into, away from, or across the direction of the tide.* It can't do anything but just go along for the ride. It does not move in relation to the water, as there is nothing to make it move. A power boat with the engine shut off, a rowboat without oars, a Six Meter and a Moth under these circumstances will all move at the same speed, and in the same direction, in relation to the bottom, and none of them will move in relation to the water.

In the case of the power boat or the rowboat, if we start the engine or start rowing, the boat will then move in relation to the water. Its motion over the bottom can be plotted by drawing a vector representing the motion over the bottom due to the tide alone, in the proper direction with its length representing velocity, and another vector representing the motion through the water alone, in the proper direction and with a length representing the speed of motion through the water. The actual total motion over the bottom is the resultant of these two vectors, as shown in Figures 47 and 48.

This whole dissertation on the laws of motion should probably have been given earlier in the chapter, but it seemed that it might be better to give a general idea of the problems first, then to take up the specific problem of explaining the lee-bow effect, with a complete explanation. If this explanation seems too elemental, forgive me—but an awful lot of skippers with years of experience sailing in tides are going to disagree with me and I have to present an airtight defense. A number of things said earlier will be repeated on the assumption that they may not have sunk in at the time, or may not have been accepted as facts.

As mentioned earlier—the problem of plotting the motion of a sailboat sailing in the presence of tides becomes quite complicated by the fact that when the tide starts moving the boat around in relation to the bottom and in relation to the actual wind, the apparent wind moves around too. This effect would be hopelessly difficult to analyze when the boat is going to windward, except for one fact that we can safely lift from the science of aerodynamics—for any given airfoil section (or suit of sails) there is one angle to the wind which will give the maximum ratio of lift to drag, and this angle is not affected by the speed of the wind within the limits of the velocities we are working with.

This fact justifies the assumption that for any given boat and suit of sails, the boat will go best to windward with the apparent wind at a constant angle to the centerline of the boat. In Figure 50, this is shown to be 32½ degrees for a typical small sailboat for which we assumed a representative speed in relation to wind velocity. We also know that wind velocity affects the speed of the boat, but this is a very complex ratio and no attempt is made to calculate it—a guess is good enough for the purposes of illustration.

In Figures 54 through 61, the effects of tide on apparent wind and on course made good are shown by diagrams for a complete racing course, with the direction of the tide in relation to the wind going all the way around the compass. The basic relationship of boat speed and wind velocity and direction is the same as in Figure 50.

On the beat in Figure 57 we have the case where one tack is almost directly into the tide. The correctness of the statement that most of your beating should be as near as possible into the tide is shown here as the starboard tack certainly doesn't get to windward very well—but it is the effect of the tide on the direction of the apparent wind combined with the tide setting the boat to leeward that is the cause, not any so-called lee-bow effect. The same comments apply to the opposite tacks in Figure 60.

These diagrams also serve to illustrate what was meant earlier in this chapter when I said "you want to be sure that the course you are heading on is going to end you up where you want to go" and also that "the direction in which you are moving in relation to the bottom or anything tied to it may be far different." Don't forget what the lee-bow effect can do for you in taking you to windward—and also what a tide on your weather bow will do in the opposite direction when approaching a mark.

I mentioned earlier that pinching is very bad when beating directly into the tide. Pinching over a long period of time is never a good idea, but a tide on the beam setting the boat to windward lessens the effect of pinching, and there will be occasions when a

RACING WITH THE TIDE FROM THE SOUTH
AND THE WIND FROM THE NORTH

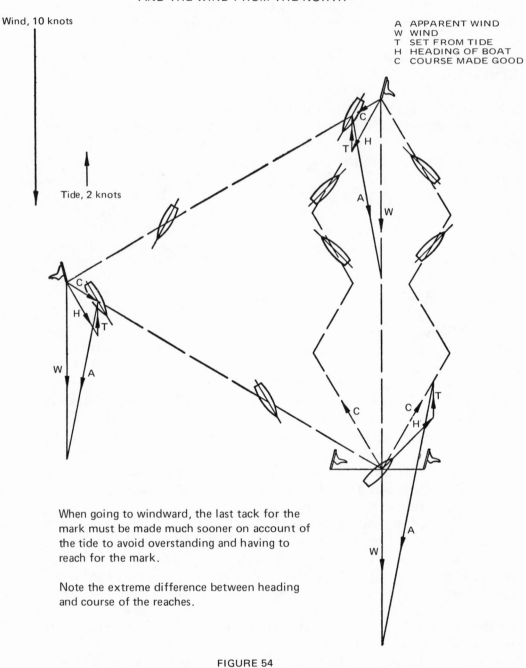

Wind, 10 knots

Tide, 2 knots

A APPARENT WIND
W WIND
T SET FROM TIDE
H HEADING OF BOAT
C COURSE MADE GOOD

When going to windward, the last tack for the mark must be made much sooner on account of the tide to avoid overstanding and having to reach for the mark.

Note the extreme difference between heading and course of the reaches.

FIGURE 54

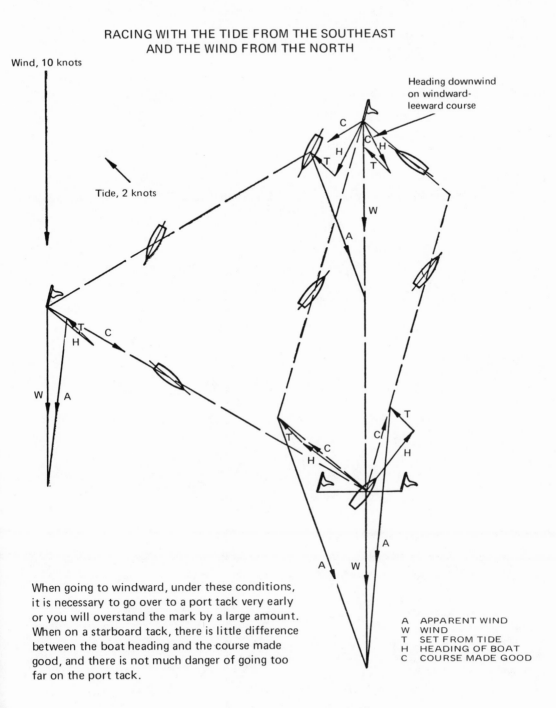

RACING WITH THE TIDE FROM THE SOUTHEAST
AND THE WIND FROM THE NORTH

Wind, 10 knots

Tide, 2 knots

Heading downwind
on windward-
leeward course

A   APPARENT WIND
W   WIND
T   SET FROM TIDE
H   HEADING OF BOAT
C   COURSE MADE GOOD

When going to windward, under these conditions,
it is necessary to go over to a port tack very early
or you will overstand the mark by a large amount.
When on a starboard tack, there is little difference
between the boat heading and the course made
good, and there is not much danger of going too
far on the port tack.

FIGURE 55

RACING WITH THE TIDE FROM THE EAST
AND THE WIND FROM THE NORTH

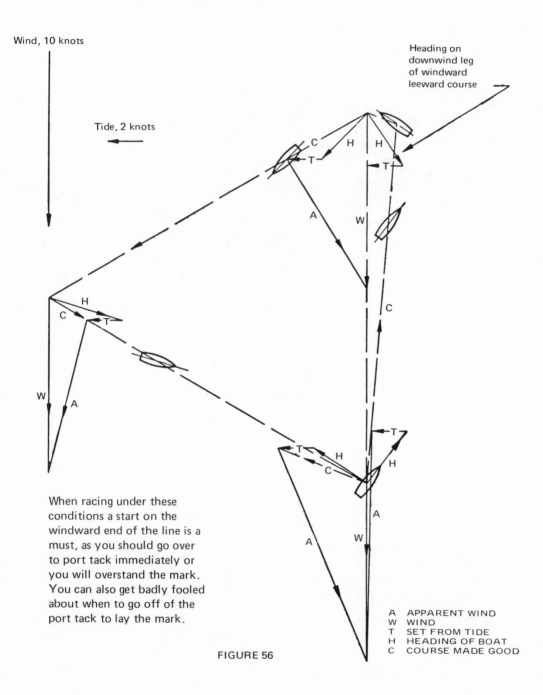

Wind, 10 knots

Heading on
downwind leg
of windward
leeward course

Tide, 2 knots

When racing under these
conditions a start on the
windward end of the line is a
must, as you should go over
to port tack immediately or
you will overstand the mark.
You can also get badly fooled
about when to go off of the
port tack to lay the mark.

A   APPARENT WIND
W   WIND
T   SET FROM TIDE
H   HEADING OF BOAT
C   COURSE MADE GOOD

FIGURE 56

RACING WITH THE TIDE FROM THE NORTHEAST
AND THE WIND FROM THE NORTH

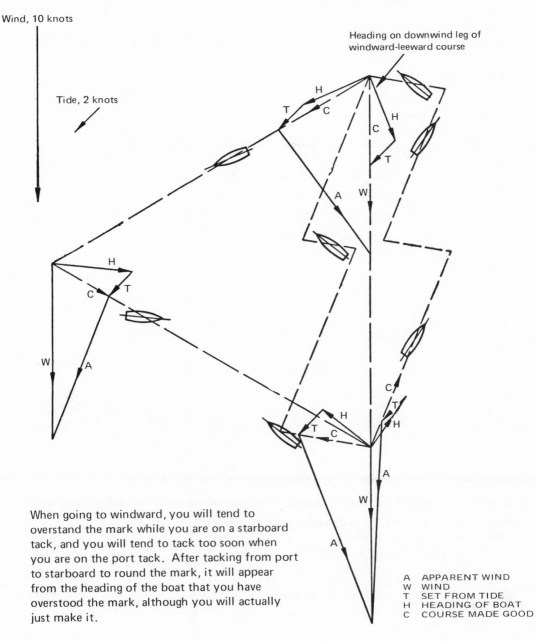

Wind, 10 knots

Tide, 2 knots

Heading on downwind leg of
windward-leeward course

When going to windward, you will tend to
overstand the mark while you are on a starboard
tack, and you will tend to tack too soon when
you are on the port tack. After tacking from port
to starboard to round the mark, it will appear
from the heading of the boat that you have
overstood the mark, although you will actually
just make it.

A   APPARENT WIND
W   WIND
T   SET FROM TIDE
H   HEADING OF BOAT
C   COURSE MADE GOOD

FIGURE 57

RACING WITH THE WIND AND TIDE
BOTH FROM THE NORTH

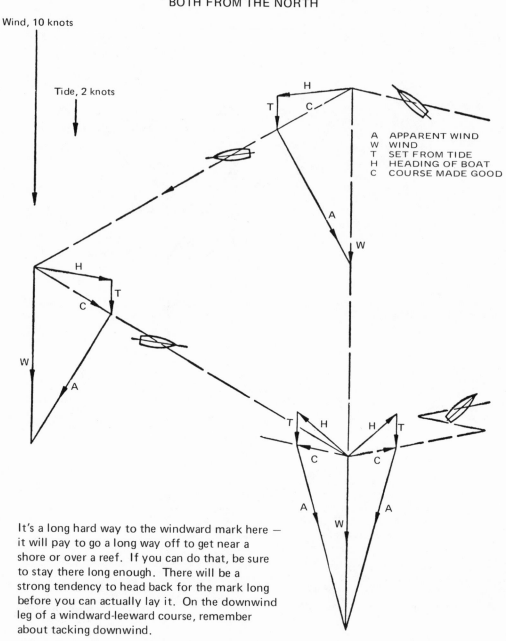

Wind, 10 knots

Tide, 2 knots

A   APPARENT WIND
W   WIND
T   SET FROM TIDE
H   HEADING OF BOAT
C   COURSE MADE GOOD

It's a long hard way to the windward mark here —
it will pay to go a long way off to get near a
shore or over a reef. If you can do that, be sure
to stay there long enough. There will be a
strong tendency to head back for the mark long
before you can actually lay it. On the downwind
leg of a windward-leeward course, remember
about tacking downwind.

FIGURE 58

RACING WITH THE TIDE FROM THE NORTHWEST
AND THE WIND FROM THE NORTH

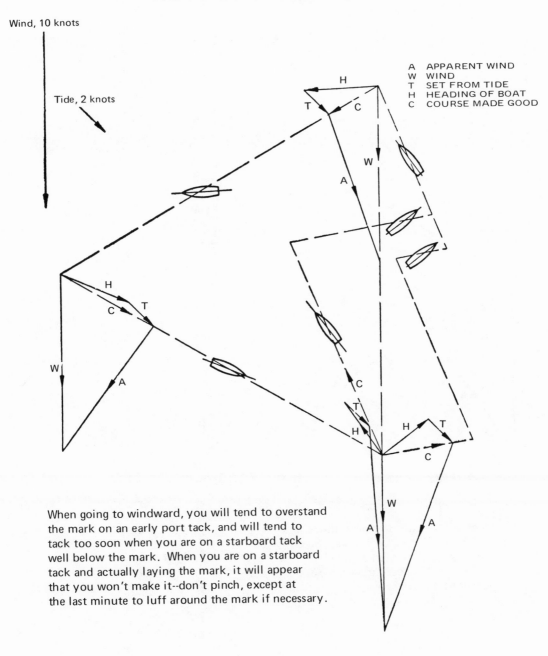

Wind, 10 knots

Tide, 2 knots

A   APPARENT WIND
W   WIND
T   SET FROM TIDE
H   HEADING OF BOAT
C   COURSE MADE GOOD

When going to windward, you will tend to overstand
the mark on an early port tack, and will tend to
tack too soon when you are on a starboard tack
well below the mark. When you are on a starboard
tack and actually laying the mark, it will appear
that you won't make it--don't pinch, except at
the last minute to luff around the mark if necessary.

FIGURE 59

RACING WITH THE TIDE FROM THE WEST
AND THE WIND FROM THE NORTH

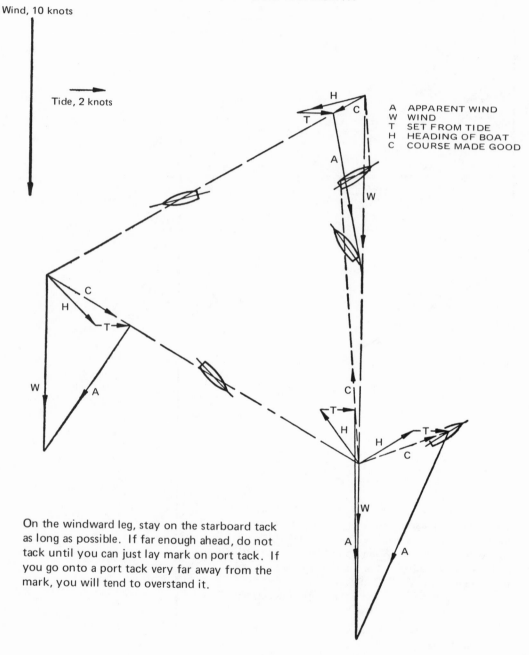

Wind, 10 knots

Tide, 2 knots

A   APPARENT WIND
W   WIND
T   SET FROM TIDE
H   HEADING OF BOAT
C   COURSE MADE GOOD

On the windward leg, stay on the starboard tack
as long as possible. If far enough ahead, do not
tack until you can just lay mark on port tack. If
you go onto a port tack very far away from the
mark, you will tend to overstand it.

FIGURE 60

RACING WITH THE TIDE FROM THE SOUTHWEST
AND THE WIND FROM THE NORTH

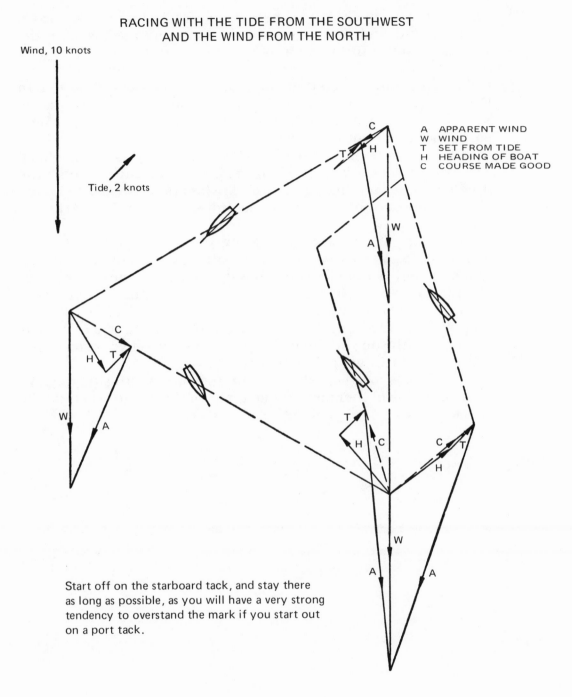

Wind, 10 knots

Tide, 2 knots

A   APPARENT WIND
W   WIND
T   SET FROM TIDE
H   HEADING OF BOAT
C   COURSE MADE GOOD

Start off on the starboard tack, and stay there
as long as possible, as you will have a very strong
tendency to overstand the mark if you start out
on a port tack.

FIGURE 61

little judicious pinching will be good tactics. In Figures 60 and 61, if you should find that you just can't quite lay the mark on the starboard tack, a little pinching will be better than coming about twice to lay the mark, particularly if there are boats behind you and to windward of you that you might not clear if you tacked. In Figure 56, if the windward mark were to be left to starboard, the same comment would apply to a boat approaching the mark on a port tack and not quite laying it.

A tide from the aft quarter has a similar but less strong effect. The starboard tack boat in Figure 54 could afford to pinch a little if he found he couldn't lay the mark when he was close to it, and also the tide as shown would make luffing around the mark a lot safer.

In Figure 59, the tide is helping the starboard-tack boat to windward to some extent, but primarily it is just slowing it down. Pinching here is probably not advisable under any circumstances, although a little might be justified at the last minute. Shooting the mark here can be quite dangerous—to a lesser degree than in Figures 57 and 58—but still to a dangerous extent, as you may clear the mark with your luff, and then have the tide set your stern onto it before you can get going on a reach.

The figures look complicated, but they are worth studying. An understanding of them will remove a lot of the mystery behind the effect of tides.

PART IV

Some Random Reflections from Experience

1

The Vagaries of Wind

No matter where you sail the wind constantly varies both in direction and velocity, the only consistency being that the lighter the wind is and the smaller the body of water over which it blows, the more it varies. There are two types of variations which must be understood before the racing skipper can hope to cope with them successfully. I don't know of any recognized scientific or technical terms for them—maybe there are some—but I will call them temporal variations and geographic variations.

Mr. Webster says temporal is "of, pertaining to, or limited by time; transitory or temporary"—which accurately describes the variations in both wind direction and velocity experienced on a small inland lake. Temporal variations exist on large bodies of water also, but generally not to the extent that they do on small ones. The lighter the average wind is the more transitory and temporary the variations are. *These temporal variations usually move across the surface of the water and generally (but not always) will eventually affect everyone in a fairly large area.*

The favorite tricks of temporal variations are to pick up all the boats in the middle of the fleet and carry them up past the leaders who are just sitting frantically smoking cigarettes, or to pick up all the boats on one tack approaching a mark, either with a shift or an increase in velocity, and take them around the mark while the erstwhile leaders on the opposite tack sit and watch the parade. The puff will get to them shortly but in the meantime their outlook on life is pretty bleak. A typical example of how screwy they can get occurs oftener than anywhere else at the Missouri Yacht Club regatta when, five minutes after starting on a beat, boats are on both tacks close-hauled, on both tacks reaching, and running with their whisker poles out on both sides, and all going in the same direction. The boys who suggest paddling back to the dock and shooting craps for the trophy have something.

Geographic variations are variations in direction and velocity *which stay put in a given location for a fairly long period of time, and do not travel across the water like the temporal ones do.* These variations are of two types—predictable ones and unpredictable ones. The predictable ones are caused by the topography of the land surrounding the water, and may occur on small or large bodies of water. The unpredictable ones generally are characteristic of large bodies of more or less open water, where there is no obvious reason to suspect any dirty work. If I knew what caused these unpredictable ones I wouldn't spend so much time being in the wrong place at the right time when racing on large bodies of water. The unpredictable ones occur rather infrequently on inland lakes and fairly frequently on large bodies of water. The predictable type exists more frequently on inland lakes simply because the lakes are smaller and you are always racing much closer to the shore line.

Unpredictable geographic wind variations can cause a lake sailor a lot of trouble when he is sailing on a large body of water, because he is likely to think that no such thing should exist when he is a long distance away from shore and the shore line has no hills or trees on it. He is accustomed to coping with geographic variations by approaching shore lines gingerly and watching carefully to see whether the boats inshore are doing better than the ones off-shore and vice versa, and staying away from windward shores, but he is likely to become a little absent-minded when he gets on a large body of water, with the result that frequently by the time he finds out that there is a geographic variation it is too late to do anything about it. Deep water sailors get caught now and then too.

In the fourth race at the Snipe National Championship on Barnegat Bay in 1951, there were a couple of geographic variations which were about as unpredictable and about as big as any I have ever seen. Shortly after getting a good start on the leeward end of a starting line which greatly favored this end of the line, I decided that I had been on a starboard tack long enough and I had better go on to a port tack to go over and stay generally between the fleet and the mark. By the time I had gone back on a starboard tack I was ahead of all of the boats that were taking a middle course, but the boats that had held the starboard tack and hadn't gone on a port tack at all were way ahead of me.

At the start of the second lap I was pretty well back in the fleet and all of the boats ahead of me except one rounded the leeward mark and started off on the starboard tack which had paid off so well on the first lap. I decided to take a short port tack merely to avoid following directly behind everyone ahead of me, and found much to my amazement, that when I went on to the starboard tack I was pointing at least 10 degrees higher than the boats which had taken a starboard tack directly away from the mark. With only a few short hitches on the port tack I was able to lay the mark on the starboard tack, moving up to second place at the second windward mark. A few of the starboard tackers either got smart after awhile and came on over, or got there accidentally as I did, but a lot of them just kept following the track that had been so successful the first lap and dropped back hopelessly, the boats which had been in the lead going back to about the middle of the fleet.

On another occasion in the Midwinter Regatta at Clearwater, Florida, we were racing in the Gulf and all the smart skippers knew that because of the tide, the only thing to do was to hold the starboard tack along the shore until you could lay the windward mark, then go out to sea. Carlos Bosch goofed on timing his start by an even 30 seconds, so he started with his wind clear but could see no future in following the starboard-tack parade. After going about a third as far as he should have gone on the port tack, he caught a geographical variation that let him tack and lay the windward mark. Various other tail enders peeled off the starboard parade down the shore and followed him around the mark, with the erstwhile leaders wondering who these jerks were sailing around the windward mark as if they were in the race. They were too far away to tell who it was leading the race that they thought they were leading. It didn't work the second lap.

On the other hand, there are predictable variations that can be very profitable. Buzz Lamb tells the following story: in a more recent Midwinter Regatta that was held on Tampa Bay, the wind was fairly light and from a southerly direction. In an afternoon race, I got off to a bad start and didn't seem to make much improvement. On the last downwind leg, I detected a slight shift to the west. Rounding the mark in the middle of the fleet, I held a long port tack, noting a gradual heading. When I could stand it no longer, I tacked and found myself alone—the rest of the fleet was on the other side of the course. But I had a good slant on the finish line and eventually got lifted to it without having to tack. Only one boat was far enough ahead to be able to work back and finish ahead of me. The phenomenon was, of course, the sea breeze. As the land warms up, the air over it rises and pulls cooler wind in from the ocean. It is quite predictable in places like Florida.

The answer seems to be that you can never afford to just look for temporal variations, and if there aren't any, assume that you can sail along watching the scenery. If you do, the scenery is likely to suddenly consist of boats now ahead of you that you had written off long ago.

Also, when one of these geographic variations exists, you had better detect its existence early in the race and get over there and take advantage of it as soon as you realize it is present instead of staying where you are and hoping that it will eventually get over to you. They just don't move across the water the way that temporal shifts do—you have to go to them.

An especially exasperating geographical variation may be encountered in light winds on the run directly before the wind on an Olympic course. This involves a streak or streaks of wind of higher-than-average velocity extending a very short distance laterally across the course but for a very long distance downwind. If you notice boats across the wind from you going faster than you think they should, keep your eye on them. If they slow down in a moment, it was just a puff and you can forget it. If they keep coming, they are probably in a streak which will remain very narrow in width but may last the entire length of the leg of the course. The streak is not going to come to you—you will have to go to it. Conversely, if you are in a streak, stay there by heading dead downwind instead of towards the mark for as long as you can.

2

When in Rome

THE OLD ADAGE WHICH RECOMMENDS COPYING THE ACTIONS OF THE local boys when you are away from home has its limitations when an attempt is made to apply it to sailing under widely varying conditions. There are two basic problems which must be separated in order to get the answer. One pertains to tactics as affected by tricky local conditions in which local skippers may have an advantage due to their intimate knowledge with these local conditions. The other involves the difference in technique between sailing on large bodies of water with big waves and on small bodies of water with no waves.

LOCAL TACTICS

The value of knowledge about local conditions is pretty generally overrated. Usually any smart skipper would figure out most of the things for himself, and usually the problem is that you get so much advice concerning local conditions that you don't know which to ignore and which to follow. I have actually run into only a few cases where it was necessary to plan tactics on the basis of local advice. One of these cases was in Long Beach, California, where both in 1950 and 1956, it was almost always necessary to go on a port tack immediately after the start, and stay there until you either ran into a sea wall and had to go on a starboard tack until you could get on a port tack again, or without a sea wall, just hold the port tack until you could tack for the mark. The only time you didn't have to do this was on the very rare occasions when the wind was very light and shifty, when you had to tack on the shifts. With a light but steady breeze, you had to get in the groove. A similar condition seemed to exist in Havana when sailing inside the harbor. I was never able to figure out any logical reason why these conditions should exist, but they did.

At Green Lake, Wisconsin, they have one course in which the windward mark is just off of a cove, and the port-tack approach is under a very high bluff and close to it. Any fool could plainly see that the way to sail that course would be to stay out in the lake, and come into the mark on a starboard tack. Only it doesn't work that way. If the port tack is parallel to the shore, or nearly so, the stupid port tacker gets to the windward mark hundreds of feet ahead of his smarter competitor who does things the way he is supposed to.

LOCAL TECHNIQUES

The problems pertaining to technique which face the inland lake skipper the first time he gets on a large body of water with big waves and the problems facing the skipper accustomed to sailing on large bodies of water when he first tries lake sailing are just about equally difficult to solve.

With large waves and fairly good wind the lake sailor will not be too badly off going to windward; however, when he starts on a reach or a run he will think he has his anchor dragging. If he runs into a heavy chop or large waves with a fairly light wind he won't even be able to go to windward. On the other hand, the average deep-water sailor having to cope for the first time with some of the things that are just normal on Missouri Yacht Club's Lake Lotawana, or Wichita's Santa Fe Lake, will be a likely candidate for a straitjacket to wear on his way to the padded cell.

Trying to do as the Romans do isn't very helpful in either case, as the skipper out of his accustomed surroundings can't see that anyone else is doing things any differently than the way he is doing them.

Practice is the only thing that will enable a skipper to master the widely different techniques required, but here are some pointers on where to focus your attention while trying to learn.

SAILING ON LARGE BODIES OF WATER

The technique for making a boat go to windward in high waves or heavy chop is logical and sounds easy—it simply involves not pointing too high. Unfortunately, in practice the lake sailor will find that it doesn't work quite as easily as it sounds and it takes quite a lot of experience to be able to master the technique. It is particularly difficult when the waves or chop exist in a moderate wind.

When I went to Havana in 1950 I had sailed in four regattas at Clearwater, Florida; three at Corpus Christi, Texas; and one in Long Beach, California, and thought I knew the answers pretty well when it came to handling waves. However, in two of the races in Havana on the Gulf of Mexico the wind was from about 6 to 8 miles an hour and the waves about three times as high in relation to the wind velocity as I had ever seen anywhere else, and I simply couldn't make any progress to windward. While I have won the Clearwater, Florida, Midwinter Regatta six times, and the Western Hemisphere Championships of the Snipe Class there once, each time I get there after not sailing during the winter, I have an awful time when there is a heavy chop and a fairly light wind. Sometimes I manage to get back into the groove again before the regatta is over and sometimes not.

The secret of success seems to be that the amount you should bear off is very very slight and you must keep your eyes glued on the luff of the jib to be sure that you are pointing exactly where you should be. A microscopic amount too high and your boat just jumps up and down. A microscopic amount too far off the wind and you just fall off without going any faster than you would be going if you were pointing properly. You and your crew should also sit farther back on the boat than in smooth water.

As far as the technique of accomplishing this is concerned there seem to be two schools of thought. One of them maintains that the sails should not be trimmed quite as tightly, which automatically requires the skipper to bear off a little bit to keep his sails full. The other school of thought is to trim the sails where they normally would be trimmed without regard to the chop or the waves and then just keep the sails a little more full than normal by bearing off slightly. When I try the first method, the only thing I seem to accomplish is to not point quite as high as the experts and at the same time not go any faster. I seem to have better luck with the second method, but I have a lot of trouble even doing this if I haven't sailed in waves or a heavy chop for a number of months.

When the wind gets up to around 15 miles an hour or higher the lake sailor won't have quite as much trouble going to windward in waves unless they are very steep and close together, as the boat then has enough momentum so that the impact of the waves doesn't slow it down as easily; however, it is under these wind conditions when the lake sailor will have his greatest trouble going off the wind.

The first year that I went to Clearwater we sailed three races on the Gulf, all of them in winds around 15 miles an hour. I went to windward all right but on the reaches and the runs the Florida boats went by me like the Twentieth Century passing a slow freight. Running down the inside channel behind the island after the race was over (where there were no waves) I could catch all of the boats that had passed me during the race, but unfortunately they didn't give any trophies for getting back to the Yacht Club first.

I was thoroughly baffled by the whole situation as I was sure that I was handling the boat as I always had handled it and there was obviously nothing wrong with the boat or the sails, as I could catch everybody on the way home; therefore, it has to be something that I was or was not doing in the race. Ted Kemensky gave me the answer—which is to not fight the boat on a reach and a run. It also seems to pay to move back a bit from where you would sit in smooth water, sliding even farther back whenever the boat starts to surfboard on a wave.

When reaching or running in a heavy chop or fairly good-sized waves, the boat seems to want to head in practically any direction except towards the mark. The lake sailor constantly attempts to correct these tendencies with his tiller—which seems to do a wonderful job of slowing down the boat. The answer is to let the boat go dashing off wherever it wants to as long as it stays within 30 degrees or so of the average course that you want it to follow. This involves keeping the tiller absolutely motionless except when the boat goes too far off of its course or when it looks like an accidental jibe might be coming up. There are a lot of other things which must be considered, of course, but I believe that the most important thing for a lake sailor to learn is that he must practically bolt the tiller down to the deck so that it can't be moved or he will be moving it a great deal more than he should.

Some other interesting problems come up in connection with going directly downwind when the wind is blowing hard and there is either heavy chop or high waves. In considering this question, it is necessary to separate the conditions with the heavy chop from those with high waves, as the technique is entirely different. In considering what to do under these conditions, it is also necessary to decide when discretion becomes the better part of valor.

When running directly before the wind with a high wind and *small* waves, the boat will plane very fast, and with the board up may develop an uncontrollable rolling tendency. This happens frequently on protected water and is not only disconcerting, but if it goes far enough to get the end of the whisker pole in the water you have either a torn jib or a broken whisker pole—or both. You may also go for an unscheduled swim. When this situation starts to develop, caution your crew to be ready to drop the board whenever you say to. About one complete oscillation is generally enough to indicate whether trouble is coming. If it looks like things are developing rapidly, have the crew drop the board when the boat is straight up, rather than waiting until you are heeled way over one way or the other.

As the waves *start picking up* (before they get high enough to surfboard on), there will frequently occur a combination of wave spacing and height which seems to make the boat want to become a submarine and sometimes the boat practically will not plane at all. When this happens, the standard method of unburying the bow by rapidly wiggling the tiller does not always work even when the crew and skipper are sitting as far back on the boat as they can get. In this case, the only method of getting the bow back up is to slack off on the jib sheet and let the whisker pole go well forward until the bow comes up, then pull it back again. It might be added that no sane person would have the whisker pole out under these conditions. I have often wondered if it would not pay to head far enough into the wind so that the boat would really plane rather than holding a straight course for the mark. This, of course, would mean an extra jibe and would necessitate traveling quite a bit of extra distance, but I have a suspicion that it would pay off.

When the waves are high enough so that the boat is surfboarding on the top of the waves when going downwind, the centerboard should be carried about as high up as you can get it, even though this increases the rolling tendency of the boat. The reason for this is that when the wave on which you are surfboarding decides to break, it practically throws the boat forward and the boat has a very strong tendency to switch ends. If it starts to switch ends and the board is down, you are over before you can do anything about it. If the board is up, the boat will merely slide sideways long enough for you to get things under control.

SAILING ON SMALL LAKES

As far as technique is concerned the deep-sea sailor will probably not have much trouble on lakes as long as the wind blows about 15 miles an hour or more. He will find that he can point a little bit higher than he is accustomed to, and he should sit a little bit farther forward in the boat on reaches and runs than he is accustomed to when reaching and running on large waves. He should tack much more frequently than on a large body of water. When the wind gets light his problems increase rapidly. The wind will vary considerably in velocity with the result that the sails must be constantly retrimmed if the sheets are cleated, or if they are not cleated the tension on the sheet must be in correct relationship to the wind velocity.

The actual position to which the sails should be trimmed when on a beat does not change with different wind velocities, but if the sails are trimmed properly for a 7- or 8-mile-an-hour wind, they will automatically be trimmed too flat when the wind drops to 3 or 4 miles an hour unless the position of the sheet is changed because there is not as much wind pressure stretching the sails themselves and the sheets. When the wind picks up again in another minute or two the sails will have to be trimmed in again because the higher pressure will cause more stretch in the sails and in the sheets.

On a reach in a light wind it will generally pay to bear off somewhat in the stronger puffs and head up somewhat in the periods when the wind has dropped. For small variations, you might just as well hold your course, but in any case the trim of the sails will probably not remain constant for over a few seconds at a time if you are going to get the maximum performance out of the boat. Keep your sheets as slack as you can and still hold the sails full. The amount that the sheets are slacked off or trimmed in will be much greater on a reach than on a beat because on a reach, the position of the sail is changed; on a beat the sails are kept in the same place, the tension on the sheets being changed only enough to keep the sails where they belong. In very light winds the crew weight should be shifted farther forward. When going to windward the boat should be pointed as high as possible without the jib luffing, and in fact with some jibs, the boat should be sailed with a slight luff in the jib all the time. The difference between pointing too high and not high enough is very small and constant attention is required.

Luck always plays some part in the winning of sailing races, and in races on small inland lakes in light winds, luck can play a big part. The important thing is to recognize this fact and not worry about it if you seem to be having lots of luck and all of it bad. The chances are that the breaks will even out pretty well in the end if you just relax and sail as well as you can; just don't write off everything that happens to you as bad luck without being sure that lady luck wasn't helped a bit by dumbness or a lack of alertness on your part.

Another good time to relax is on the start when the wind is very light and shifty. A perfect start is not worth too much under these conditions, as those behind can watch the leaders and profit by their mistakes. I don't mean to recommend throwing away your stopwatch under these conditions, but if you are a little late on the start, have your boat moving and your wind clear and you are just as well off or maybe better than if you are out in front trying to cover the whole fleet. Sounds crazy but it seems to work this way.

The big problem in lake sailing is deciding when to tack on a shift and when not to. When the wind is more than about 5 miles an hour, it is generally best to wait several seconds after a shift seems to have occurred to be sure that the shift has actually occurred, and then tack. After tacking, make an immediate check on the new course to be sure that the shift has stayed with you. When the wind velocity is in the range of 5 to 15 miles an hour, very frequent tacking will be necessary to take full advantage of all the temporal shifts which will occur. The decision on when to tack and when not to will cause the deep-sea sailor lots of trouble.

When the wind is around 3 or 4 miles an hour and occasionally drops to practically nothing, it is very difficult to decide what to do. You know that your jib has collapsed, but you don't know whether it has collapsed because there simply isn't any wind and your boat is still going on momentum or because the wind shifted. With this kind of a wind you will generally have a cigarette going to serve as a wind indicator, and the smoke coming from your cigarette can serve to give you a slightly more educated guess as to whether the wind has actually shifted or whether it has merely died. When your jib starts to collapse, look at the cigarette smoke and bear off a little bit in the effort to get your jib to fill. If the jib does not fill, and if the cigarette smoke shows that the wind is still coming from directly ahead, this probably means that the wind has merely died, and you might as well hold your original direction until you either run out of momentum or the wind picks up.

This may involve sailing for a fair length of time with the jib completely collapsed. However, if you attempt to keep the jib filled by bearing off, and your trouble is actually that the wind has simply died, you will find yourself going around in a circle, and assuming that the wind comes back from the direction from which it was originally blowing you have lost a lot of progress to windward. If you decide to tack under these circumstances you will have a hard time getting about, you will lose all your momentum in the process, and will probably just succeed in getting about by the time the wind comes back up and you will have to tack again.

The geographic variations in wind on an inland lake can generally be predicted fairly well. When the wind is blowing off the shore it is not a good idea to go too close to the shore. If the shore happens to be a high bank or have high trees, it will pay to stay a long way out from it. On a reach there will be a strong temptation to go close to the shore because the boats near the shore get the puffs of wind earlier and look momentarily like they are making better progress. The only thing to do is to make up your mind as to how far off-shore you think you should be, and then stay there. If you start changing your mind frequently as to where you should be, you will generally find out that every place you go you have gotten there just after the wind left.

When the wind is parallel to a shore line, the situation gets tricky and unpredictable. Sometimes you don't dare go in towards shore, and sometimes you don't dare not to. All you can do is to experiment cautiously and watch other boats carefully. Any variation that is found can generally be considered a geographic variation and the condition will usually exist for some time.

Considerably higher winds can be handled on small inland lakes, and in many cases these winds will be very gusty. Just be a bit careful on luffing the puffs when going to windward.

3

Using a Compass in Racing

A GREAT MANY PEOPLE SEEM TO BE BAFFLED ON THE SUBJECT OF USING a compass in connection with small-boat racing, some of them being baffled as to why one should be used and some as to how. A compass is obviously not essential on a small boat as people have been winning races without one for years—there are, however, some occasions on which a compass is very helpful.

An experienced skipper can reach down a starting line and harden up on the wind and guess pretty well which end of the line will be the best end to start on without using a compass. However, in the excitement that prevails immediately before a start, he is likely to get caught starting on the wrong end of the line if the wind has shifted appreciably since he tried the starting line. A compass may help to avoid this. With a compass the first thing you do is to get the compass reading when reaching down the starting line on a starboard tack. In the illustration (Figure 62) the compass reading in this case is 180 degrees. Then if the compass reading when close-hauled on a starboard tack is over 45 degrees more than the starting line reading (more than 225 degrees) the starboard end of the line will give the shortest course to the windward mark. If the starboard tack close-hauled is less than 45 degrees more than the starting line reading (in example, less than 225 degrees) then the port end of the line will give the shortest course. Sometimes considerations other than the shortest course will govern in deciding which end of the line to pick, as covered earlier in this book.

In a high wind it is a good idea to keep an eye on the starting

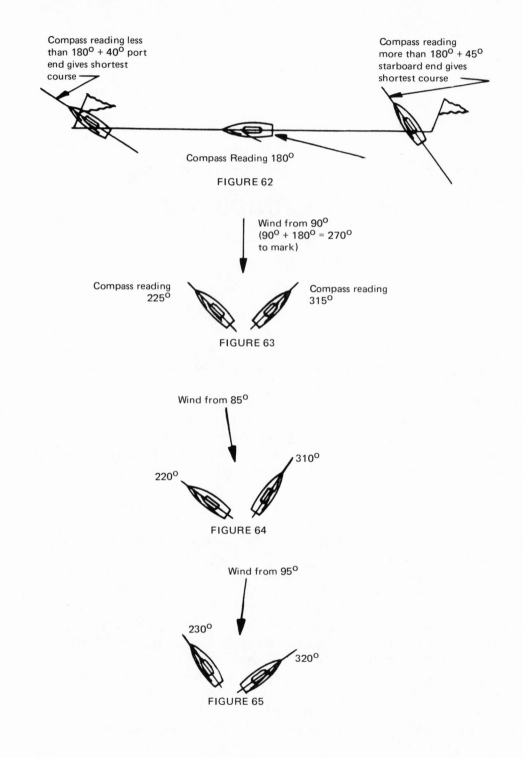

Compass reading less than 180° + 40° port end gives shortest course

Compass reading more than 180° + 45° starboard end gives shortest course

Compass Reading 180°

FIGURE 62

Wind from 90°
(90° + 180° = 270°
to mark)

Compass reading 225°

Compass reading 315°

FIGURE 63

Wind from 85°

310°

220°

FIGURE 64

Wind from 95°

230°

320°

FIGURE 65

markers to be sure that they aren't shifting around; however, assuming that they are not, it is only necessary to remember the compass heading of the starting line and compare this with your starboard tack heading as you maneuver before the start. If you do this, a pronounced shift in the wind will not catch you starting where you wouldn't have if you had known better.

Probably the greatest usefulness for the compass, however, is in detecting shifts when going to windward and in making sure that you haven't gotten caught tacking on an apparent shift which wasn't an actual one. In the second example (Figure 63), the wind is coming from a direction of 90 degrees which means that a straight course to the mark would be 270 degrees, the normal starboard-tack heading would be 225 degrees, and the port-tack heading would be 315 degrees. This, of course, represents an average condition as the wind never blows from exactly the same direction for very long. The actual conditions would probably be that the starboard tack varied from about 220 to 230 degrees and the port tack from about 310 to 320 degrees, as shown in Figures 64 and 65. Obviously, when the starboard-tack heading is 230 degrees you are heading closer to the mark than on the port tack with a heading of 320 degrees. Conversely, when the port-tack heading is 310 degrees you are heading closer to the mark than on a starboard tack with a heading of 220 degrees.

Deciding when to tack and when not to tack involves a lot more than merely reading the compass. However, it is generally true that you should be on the tack which heads closest to the mark, and using a compass will enable you to determine this. It will also enable you to determine whether or not you have gotten caught tacking on an apparent shift.

If, for instance, you have been holding the starboard tack with a heading of 230 degrees, and your heading suddenly drops to 220 degrees, it will pay to come about. If you have come about on an actual shift, your port-tack heading will be 310 degrees. If, however, you have tacked on an apparent shift your port heading will be 320 degrees and you had better get back where you were.

The most dangerous thing about using a compass while racing is that it is easy to become so engrossed in doing what the compass says to do that you may forget to watch the other boats carefully enough. This may cause you to completely miss the presence of a geographic shift when going to windward, and may cause you to forget that while a compass course to the next mark on a reach or a run may be the shortest distance to the mark, going off course to stay ahead of your most dangerous competitor may get you to the mark ahead of him instead of behind him.

4

Going to Windward

IN LOOKING OVER THE CORRESPONDENCE FOR ANY PERIOD, I HAVE NOTICED that a fair percentage of the letters that I receive are from skippers wanting to get to the windward mark sooner than they have been doing. The specific questions are sometimes, "How can I make my boat point higher?", "My boat points high in light wind but won't in a high wind (and vice-versa). What can I do about it?", "In our fleet, boats made by X point higher than boats made by Y, what can I do about it?", and from another part of the country, "In our fleet, boats made by Y point higher than boats made by X, what can I do about it?"

Almost everything that will be said here has been written earlier in this book, but maybe it will help to get it all pulled together in one place. In the first place—you have to start with the boat.

1. Are your mast and centerboard properly located and with enough mast rake so that you have practically no weather helm? Do you have the right amount of slack in your rigging?
2. Do you have free-running blocks and easily operated cleats?
3. Is the bottom smooth and fair? Same for the centerboard and rudder? Is the slot in the keel where the centerboard passes through it fitted closely to the board?
4. Do you have a mainsheet traveler which will permit you to strap down the main without pulling the boom in too far? And pinching strings?
5. Do you have hiking straps for both the skipper and the

crew? a tiller which is long enough to permit you to sit fairly well forward but not so long that it gets in your way when coming about? And do you have a tiller extension?

6. Is your boat at minimum weight?
7. Do you have good sails?
8. Do your sails fit the stiffness of your mast?
9. Have you done sufficient boat-for-boat testing?

If the answer to any of the above is no, the remedy is fairly obvious. Getting to the windward mark first depends primarily on the skipper, but there is no point in handicapping yourself!

The location of the jib fairlead, for example, depends on your mast bend characteristics as well as the jib you are using. Most jibs trim properly quite far in from the sheer but some should be on a track near the sheer. In any case, it is necessary to have fore-and-aft adjustment and sufficient testing should be done to know where the fairlead should be located for varying wind conditions. Remember that in a high wind the mast bends and the whole rig moves aft, and this means that the fairlead should be farther forward than it is in light wind for the same jib.

You must have free-running blocks and cleats that can easily be operated. If your lines hang up, you just cannot tack without losing too much time. The wind strength always varies and frequently it will be necessary to change the adjustments of the sheet very slightly, due to the varying wind velocities—and by slightly, I mean adjustments as small as a quarter of an inch on the amount the sheet is trimmed in. On jam cleats for the jib, locate them so the crew can hang onto the jib sheet in high winds without the sheet popping out of the cleats.

The proper place to trim the main on any type of boat depends to some extent on the make of sails used, and this should be determined by experiment or by copying successful skippers in your class. The traveler used should be one which will permit strapping down the sails tightly enough so that the leech does not fall off without pulling the boom in any farther than it should be, and "pinching strings" or the equivalent must be available to take care of light winds.

Some people have gone a little overboard on the subject of tiller length. I have seen some, including a French boat which I borrowed at San Remo, Italy, on which the tiller was so long that the skipper had a tendency to get tangled up in it in coming about. If you want to sit that far forward, the best thing to do is to chop off the tiller until it doesn't interfere with you while coming about and then use a longer extension.

How much difference weight makes is very debatable, but I don't think that anyone will argue that a heavy boat has any advantage. If I had to choose between a good crew weighing 190 pounds and a fairly good one weighing 140 pounds, I would take the good one with the 50-pound weight disadvantage even in a light wind. I have also decided that the advantages to be gained from the use of a heavier centerboard have been considerably exaggerated. A lighter board is much easier to handle and gives an easy way to save some pounds. Also, with a well-finished boat I do not worry at all about the amount of weight that the boat picks up as a result of being left in the water for a short time like overnight at a regatta; however, I also don't see any point in giving odds to anyone else by trying to race a boat that weighs more than the minimum.

On the subject of sails, I am becoming more and more convinced that knowing how to use a suit of sails and developing confidence in them is more important than small variations in the cut of the sails. Obviously, no one can win races with poor sails and it pays to buy the best sails that you can get; however, the leeches of all sails flutter a little bit, the jib will backwind the luff of the main on any full or medium sail, and in a very light wind, even a perfectly cut sail will probably develop a few wrinkles. If your sails are obviously no good, throw them away or keep them for moonlight sailing. If they have been made by a good sailmaker and have not been blown out of shape, stick with them and learn how to use them.

So now, you have done everything to your boat that needs to be done, and have good sails: What next? The answer to that is easy on paper—practice and lots of it. If your sailing water has turned into a mud flat as Wichita's Santa Fe Lake does occasionally, or if you live too far from your anchorage to sail evenings, this may be difficult, but practice is all important. And by practice, I don't mean just wandering around. If there is another boat that you can practice with (or against) so much the better, but you and your crew can do a lot by yourself. The standard complaint of the wife of a good racing skipper is "you never do any pleasure sailing— you're always pretending you're racing." Sad, but true—or it ought to be if you really want to win races.

It is pretty hard to tell when your boat is doing its best when there is no other boat around with which to compare your speed, but you can get lots of practice trying to keep it headed on a beat, just far enough off the wind to keep the jib full.

Whenever possible, try to practice with another boat with which you are evenly matched. Take turns sailing to windward, several boat lengths apart so neither is interfering with the wind of the other boat, but close enough so there will be no significant differences in wind velocity. One boat should experiment with changes in trim of the sails or changes in heading while the other tries to keep everything as constant as possible. This is a good place to find the perfect curvature for the foot of the jib, changing the trim of the sheet by ⅛ or ¼ of an inch, and the perfect place to trim the main. It can be done while racing too, but it is hard to tell then whether you gained because you did something right or because the other skipper did something wrong. He may have been fiddling with things too. In any case—don't forget that when going to windward, your eyes belong on the luff of the jib—not on the scenery.

If there is a good breeze, practice luffing through the puffs, and don't stay on shore just because the wind is high. In most places —particularly at regattas—you will have to race at least part of the time in high winds, and it is on these occasions that lack of practice really shows up.

Coming about needs constant practice, especially since the relatively recent advent of roll-tacking, which has been described in the chapter on Boat Handling. The advantages of roll-tacking are that the sails are filled and driving the boat during most of the time the boat is coming about, and there is an appreciable increase in wind velocity over the sails induced by the roll. The disadvantages are that the centerboard is operating at a greatly increased angle of attack induced by the lateral movement during the roll, and too quick a roll will result in a stalled airflow over the sails. Both of these actions increase drag and are the reason why considerable practice and coordination of skipper and crew are necessary for most effective use of the technique.

I suspect that this technique will come under increasing scrutiny of the regulatory authorities as a possible violation of the rule on means of propulsion. At the present time the only recognition it gets is Appendix 2 which states "frequent quickly-repeated gybing or roll-tacking in calm or near calm conditions shall fall in the same category as 'pumping' " (which is a no-no always, as is rocking). The implication here is that if you don't tack any oftener than you would have if you had never heard of roll-tacking, you are not violating the rules.

Except in a drifter when you will have to pump the boat around with the tiller (see Appeal Decision 56 for limitations on tiller movement to stay legal), and in a high wind and waves when you will find yourself in irons if you are not careful, you can just turn the tiller loose and the boat will get itself around somehow. If your mainsheet bridle is properly located, the boat will do a reasonably good job of it part of the time and a perfect job some of the time, but most of the time a little attention on the part of the skipper will result in a better job of coming about.

Have your crew watch the luff of the jib and turn loose of the sheet as soon as the luff shakes. This will be a little while after the skipper has moved the tiller, as the turning and rolling of the boat will keep the jib full for a short time. A good healthy jerk on the opposite sheet will start the jib over. In very light winds, it is possible to get the jib around quickly enough to be backwinded—which, of course, is bad—but otherwise it is only an exceptionally fast crew that can get the jib over too fast. The jib should still be fluttering when it is cleated down—if you can get it there that fast.

In general, come about on as large a radius as you can. Starting upward in the range of wind velocities from the pumping process necessary in drifting matches, the next step is to give the tiller a fairly good shove, let it stay at the limit of the travel for a moment, then ease it back to the center of the boat. A perfect job will be when you get the tiller back where it belongs at the instant that the jib fills.

The next step up, which means in winds of about 8 to 12 miles an hour, the tiller should not go all the way over to the stop. Move it over fairly slowly, hold it there an instant or so, then bring it back to the center. Again—you will have done the job perfectly if your tiller is centered at the instant that the jib fills. With winds of from 12 to 15 miles an hour on up, you can start just letting the tiller go until it hits its stop (assuming that you have a mainsheet traveler that limits its travel to about what it should be) then pull it back. In very high winds, the whole performance will be accomplished as rapidly as possible—the speed at which it is accomplished gradually increasing from a leisurely pace at a wind velocity of 15 miles an hour up to not quite fast enough no matter how you try at a wind velocity of 35 miles an hour or over.

If you have a new crew, he will probably have trouble stepping or sitting on the sheet that he isn't pulling on while in the process of coming about. A temporary expedient until he has more experience is to have him throw the sheet overboard on the far side of the boat instead of merely dropping it when he starts to pull the jib over. After you have completed the tack, don't forget to retrieve the end of the sheet which is dragging in the water. It won't slow you down much but it looks sloppy.

In high waves, try to wait for a moment when the waves are less high (waves generally come in groups and this usually happens), but in any case, don't crash into a wave while coming about if you can help it. Bear off a little just before you hit the wave, then as soon as the boat starts to move, slam the tiller over as hard as you can so that, if possible, you have things under control on the new tack before the next wave hits you.

Speaking of chop and waves, the technique given earlier will get the job done, if you have had enough practice to master it. The finest job of sailing in a heavy chop that I have ever seen was done by Clark King in the Snipe National Championship off of Alamitos Bay in Long Beach Harbor in 1956. The chop was made up of a very confused wave system coming from three directions at once, the wind was moderate, and the hotshots from all parts of the United States except California might as well have stayed home. There wasn't anything mysterious about what Clark did—he merely held the boat absolutely flat, bore off just the right amount at the right time, and kept his main trimmed perfectly all of the time. Immediately after the start, I was close enough to watch him, but not for long. I did everything he did but I didn't do it as well —nor did anyone else.

5

Just Plain High Winds

CONSIDERABLE SKEPTICISM IS SOMETIMES POLITELY EVIDENCED WHEN I write about sailing in winds of 35 miles an hour average velocity. The plain truth is that if you live in the center of the United States, and Wichita especially, you may not do any sailing before September if you wait for the wind to get under 25 miles an hour—which is considered just a nice invigorating breeze in these parts.

In the first place, sailing in these winds is only practical where the water is sheltered enough so that the waves do not become dangerous, but those people who have inadequate bailing equipment and who stop sailing when their boats take on a lot of water won't get by here either, as you can take on lots of water in a high wind even with waves only 2 or 3 feet high. Racing under these conditions is just like any other racing—you have to have proper equipment and experience to be successful. Boats that are too lightly built or rigged will fall apart. And skippers who have always sat on shore when the wind blows will probably capsize. The experts will now and then too, but not so often. Put on the smallest, flattest mainsail you have. Drop your boom as far as you can, or reef if you can.

The photograph of a Snipe in Figure 66 illustrates what can happen on a small body of water in a high wind. At first glance, nothing seems to be going on. The skipper and crew are not hiked out, the boat is not heeling at all, and everything looks peaceful. Actually the wind is blowing about 35 miles per hour on Lake Hefner at Oklahoma City during one of their Boat Clubs' spring regattas. Oklahoma City has the record for no-race regattas in this

FIGURE 66
PLANING AT THE NAUTICAL EQUIVALENT OF SUPERSONIC SOUND

part of the country—two years when the wind never got under 40 during daylight hours so no races. We might have been pushing the Snipe Sanctioned Regatta maximum wind limits a bit in the race when the photo was taken. Lake Hefner is about 2 miles in diameter and not too shallow so there were no waves of any consequence and at that time the lake had nothing around it to scramble up the wind so planing conditions were ideal.

Actually, the boat is practically flying at the nautical equivalent of supersonic speed. I've never gone as fast on a sailboat before or since. The boat had achieved a sort of dynamic stability. We did not have to hike out to hold it flat but we had an insecure feeling like sitting on a greased ball on top of a flagpole. The strength of the wind is evidenced by the extreme twist in the main, even with a four-part vang as tight as it could be pulled. The boom is at the middle stripe.

Close examination of the photo shows the chines to be quite far out of the water, which means there is not much boat in the water; there is no sign of a bow wave or stern wave and practically no wake. The spray is coming from the front edge of the centerboard which has to be out of the water to create the spray pattern shown. My crew, Jim Beddow, and I remarked at the time that nobody would believe our story and there is never a photographer around at a time like this. Two weeks later at another regatta, Bill Kilpatrick showed up with the picture, blown up to 11″ by 14″ plus mat, and said an amateur photographer who was fishing from a rowboat that day brought him the print and asked him if he thought the guy in the picture would pay ten dollars for it.

When planing directly before the wind in relatively smooth water with the centerboard up, the boat will sometimes start an uncontrollable roll. Trim the mainsail in fast and if that doesn't stop the rolling, drop your centerboard. The initial roll is caused by a high-level puff hitting the top of the sail. Even with a powerful boom vang this puff will twist the top of the sail forward of a 90-degree athwartship position, resulting in a thrust to windward at the top of the mast. Because of its leverage, this produces a strong rolling tendency which can cause a capsize to windward if you are not alert, and will certainly start an oscillation which may become violent.

This rolling not only gives one a very insecure feeling, but if allowed to go far enough so that the whisker pole gets into the water, it can tear the lashing of your jib loose or it can break your whisker pole and shoot the remaining parts through the jib, if the pole is made of wood or it will bend a metal pole. When this rolling starts, the smartest thing is not to wait and see whether it is going to be bad, but to assume it is and take necessary action.

When going directly before the wind with certain wave conditions, the boat will tend to bury itself occasionally instead of planing as you would expect it to. Under these circumstances, with the jib out on the whisker pole or the spinnaker set, the last-resort way to stop this submarining tendency is to let the pole go forward so the jib or spinnaker loses its drive. When these conditions exist secure the sheet to something so that if it is popped free from its normal trim position, it will let the sail go far enough forward to get the boat back under control, but not far enough so that you lose the pole. If you have a very light mast with shroud attachments at the deck which are not as far behind the mast as they should be, the whole rig-mast, boom, pole, shrouds, and sails may just go over the bow. Blocks behind the mast at the deck or a forward puller may help.

When going to windward, the important thing is to always keep the boat moving. Pull the mainsheet bridle down fairly flat, leave the boom vang on, and let the main out a little. Move your jib fairleads out some, and as a last resort move them aft. Don't tack unless you have enough way to keep from going into irons. When tacking off of a reach, head up onto a beat and get things set before tacking. This is particularly important in tacking for the line at the start. If the wind is very gusty, use a little discretion in luffing into the puffs going to windward.

As I said before, even experienced skippers who race frequently in high winds are going to capsize occasionally. I average once a year. I suppose skippers who have never capsized should do it on purpose to get some practice righting the boat now that most boats have sail-away capability after capsizing and righting. It really would not be too bad an idea. In any case a capsize and righting routine should be developed with your crew.

In the normal capsize to leeward, the crew should immediately go over onto the centerboard while the skipper slides into the water. The sheets should be uncleated and when battle for survival conditions are likely to exist, I have a line tied to the post at the back of the centerboard trunk which the crew is supposed to grab as he goes overboard. This line gives him something to hang onto as he stands on the end of the centerboard. If he goes over without it the skipper can toss it to him. Centerboard travel should be limited so there is at least a foot or so sticking out to stand on.

In this year's capsize we were on a beat so the board was all the way down. I had a new crew who had never sailed in high wind and he only weighed 115 pounds, but he followed the routine we had discussed and stood on the end of the board with the line in his hand until the boat started to come up. I stayed in the water hanging onto the edge of the cockpit close to the aft end of the cockpit until the boat was almost level. My crew had been gradually getting aboard as the boat came up—not too fast or it will keep on going. When the boat was almost level, I climbed on board, pulled the crew the rest of the way in, and we started off on a broad reach sitting well aft to facilitate draining. The boat is pretty unstable when first righted and you have to be careful not to start the whole process over again.

Never get both skipper and crew on the board because when the boat does come up, it will do so too fast and will just keep right on going. If you can't right the boat and need power-boat help, use the line you have tied to the aft end of the centerboard trunk. Pass this line over your boat to the power boat which should be on the side of your boat opposite the mast. Tie your line to one from the power boat if yours is not long enough. Have them pull directly across your boat slowly and your mast will start to come up. Be ready to crawl in before the boat is completely righted so you can stop it when it is upright.

Obviously you should have had your life preserver vests on before the whole procedure started.

When battle-for-survival conditions exist, an exception should be made to the procedure for jibing the downwind mark given in the chapter on Boat Handling, which recommended having the board all the way down. This recommendation was because it is very difficult to get the board down after you have started to windward. The disadvantage in jibing with the board down when a large change in course is made is that the boat tends to heel badly on completion of the jibe even if everything is properly trimmed. If the centerboard is up halfway or more, the boat will slide sideways a bit instead of heeling so much and things are under a lot better control, but if your next leg is to windward you have to get the board down somehow. Under these circumstances, I believe it is safest to go off course before you get to the mark so that you can jibe directly before the wind with the board down; then, after the jibe is completed and everything is under control, you can round the mark and head up on the beat.

6

Leakers

IF THERE IS ONE THING THAT ANNOYS A SKIPPER, IT IS TO TO HAVE A BOAT that leaks. But the fact remains, most boats leak. Even expensive ocean racers have leaks around the ports and through-deck bolts, usually caused by inadequate or worn caulking. Any time there is a joint or a fitting there is a possibility of a leak. Wooden boats have some advantage on this point, for as soon as the wood gets wet it swells, and tends to close up the joints. Although fiberglass will absorb minute quantities of water, it will not swell.

Most racing classes require positive flotation, usually in the form of foam. Foam will pick up water in varying degrees. If enough water accumulates in the foam the boat will become excessively heavy, which reduces its competitiveness. Consequently, most foam is installed in sealed-off compartments such as a double bottom or side tanks. This is all well and good until the compartment develops a leak, which happens all too often. All compartments should be provided with watertight inspection plates or drain plugs. Frequent inspection should be made to determine whether water is leaking into the compartments.

If water does start to collect in the compartments, the leak is very difficult to locate. If the leak develops in a double bottom it is usually at the point where the centerboard trunk is joined to the hull or where the inner hull is attached to the hull. The area around the mast step is another area likely to leak when sailing in high winds. If you have hit any hard objects with your dagger board, the aft end of the trunk is a very likely location. In any case, you can locate the leak by applying a slight air pressure to the drain or access hole, then slopping soapy water on the inside— particularly at the joints. The soapy water will bubble at the point where water will enter. It will be necessary to turn the boat over and apply the soapy water to the inside of the centerboard trunk to locate a leak from the hull to centerboard joint. The same procedure can be used with side tanks.

The best means of applying air pressure is a canister vacuum cleaner with the hose reversed. Be careful not to have too much pressure as it is possible to rupture the inner hull.

After the leak has been located, mix up a small amount of resin and cover the hole with resin, then apply a piece of glass matt. Don't forget to sand the surface around the hole or the resin will not stick. Usually your leak is just a pinhole, so only a small patch will be necessary. It is also possible to stop the leak with a sealant, a polysulfide type being the best that I have found. It is also a very good caulking compound to use when installing a fitting that needs to be watertight. If the boat is made of wood, do not use fiberglass, use the sealant.

7

FIBERGLASS REPAIRS*

YOUR FIRST THOUGHT WHEN YOU LOOK AT YOUR DAMAGED BOAT IS: "OH! My beautiful boat is dead!" Not so. It can be repaired as good as new (well, almost), which is a job that can be better done by you than many professionals.

Fiberglass hull damages usually come from altercations on the race course but they also come from a variety of other causes. The hole which brought about this chapter came from a rather unique situation. The centerboard was being carried under the trailer supported by two pieces of angle welded on the frame of the trailer. The problem was that space between the angles was designed for a 22″ centerboard and this one was a 20¼″ board.

Unfortunately, the wedge and lashing came loose and the board dropped with the leading edge forward. When it hit the pavement it jacked up one corner of the trailer with such a force that the trailer bolster broke the hull. It seems rather odd that the hull could be broken until you consider that the force was fairly well concentrated and the car was going 60 miles per hour. It was very disheartening to remove the cover and find my beautiful boat with a hole in it (Figures 67, 68).

The first step in repair was to remove the damaged part, including the gel coat that was badly crazed. This is best done with a power grinder as it is necessary to taper the edge. Care should

*This chapter was written by Buzz Lamb describing repairs he made to his boat. It was first published in the Snipe Bulletin, and is a useful guide to anyone facing a fiberglass boat repair.

THE DAMAGE:

Centerboard dropped from trailer as rig was being towed at 60 mph, striking trailer and causing trailer bolster to break the hull.

FIGURE 67

FIGURE 68

(Photos by Buzz Lamb)

THE REPAIR:

FIGURE 69

Damaged part removed; glass mat is cut and ready for application.

FIGURE 70

After patches have been applied.

FIGURE 71

Patch with Mylar covering, after gel coat has been applied.

be taken not to damage the foam under the fiberglass since it will be used as a base for laying on the patch. (See Figure 69.) If there is no foam at this point, a back-up plate of cardboard, held in place with battens and tape, should be placed on the inside of the hull behind the hole. The cardboard should be thoroughly waxed before installing. This will enable the cardboard to be readily removed after the fiberglass cures.

If the hole is inaccessible from the inside, attach several threads to the cardboard, roll it up and push it through the hole. Apply a thin coat of resin to the cardboard and guide it into place with the threads. This will give enough support to be able to apply the patch.

The next step is to cut about three pieces of mat, see Figure 69. The first one should cover the edge of the hole and the next should be slightly larger. The final one should just fit inside the edge of the good gel coat. Tape around the edges so resin will not get on the gel coat. The fastest way would be to apply the patches one at a time but before the previous one cures, otherwise, each will have to be sanded before the next one is applied.

The method of applying the patch is to put the patch on a piece of wax paper and saturate it with resin. Pick it up carefully and lay it on the back-up plate or previous patch. In order to save work, fair in the patch as best you can. Figure 70 shows the work after the patches have been applied.

So far the job has taken about a half hour. The rest is much more tedious. Although there is only a few hours work, it could take a week to complete, unless you force cure with a heat lamp.

The next step is to secure some gel coat of the same color as your boat. Most colors are fairly standard but the best place to get it is from the manufacturer of your boat as it will more nearly match. A perfect match is not possible because the color on the boat will probably have faded slightly. Mix the gel coat with a thickening agent to form a putty. Apply with a putty knife to fair in the holes in the patch. A number of applications will have to be made but remember to sand between coats. Here, try to keep off of the old gel coat when sanding. A straight edge will reveal when the patch is fair.

There will always be slight imperfections so now you should apply gel coat without the thickening agent. This is inevitably done with a brush and brings on more imperfections. To eliminate most of the sanding, lay wax paper on top of the brushed-on gel coat. Then put down a fairly stiff piece of cardboard, Mylar, or what have you. Roll this with a rubber roller. This will flatten out the brush marks. Figure 71 shows the patch with Mylar. Unfortunately, I did not use wax paper the first time and the gel coat stuck to the Mylar, in spite of a good coat of wax.

If you have done a real good job of fairing in and applying the gel coat, all that remains is to sand. The tool shown in Figure 71 came from an auto parts store. It is plastic and slightly flexible, and is great for fairing in, using 180 grit. However, the final sanding should be done with 400 wet or dry, then 600 wet or dry, all on a sanding block.

More than likely, you will sand through some of the new gel coat. This indicates that the patch was not fair, so sand until you think it is, then reapply the gel coat. This job required several gel coat applications.

The total cost of such a patching job should be about $8.00 if you have to go out and buy everything. A professional repair job would probably cost around $100, and in many cases, not be as good as the one you could do.

8

Advice to Amateur Painters

SINCE PRACTICALLY NO SMALL-BOAT SAILOR EVER STARTED PAINTING HIS boat as far before the deadline for finishing the job as he should have, the following advice is made available for racing skippers who have suddenly discovered that it is later than they thought.

Before even thinking about painting, there is a vast amount of work to do. The finish of the hull must be absolutely smooth. The surface of the wood must be smooth in the first place, with any rough spots being filled in with quick-drying hard putty. A relatively small amount of effort expended in sanding the wood will save a much greater amount of work later on. Most of you will be confronted with a boat that has already been painted so I will confine discussion to refinishing of wood (as well as fiberglass) boats. Incidentally, don't bother about taking the old paint off unless it is in a completely hopeless condition. It takes a long time to build up a good surface and if the old paint is sticking to the wood it is better to leave it.

The first step is to fill the scratches and gouges with a putty. Most marine paint companies make a glazing compound or putty. There are also many automobile glazing putties which I have used. I can't tell much difference, and am inclined to believe they are all about the same. These materials shrink on drying, so large holes will have to be filled in several installments. For the smaller scratches, I have found the best way to apply the putty is with an artist's palette knife. It is very flexible and enables you to get just enough putty over the hole without getting too much.

After doing all the filling, you have to sand the surface smooth.

In fact, it usually takes a couple of applications of putty, with sanding in between. No matter how careful you are, you seem to miss a few places. At this point you should sand the entire bottom with No. 280 wet-or-dry sandpaper. However, if any wood is showing, use regular sandpaper since water tends to raise the grain of wood. In any case, the sanding should be done with a block to make sure the surface comes out fair.

After this initial process you should paint the bottom with a flat undercoat. The paint dries rapidly and is designed to permit sanding in a very short time. This can be done with a brush, but spraying gives a better surface.

Now you are ready to sand again. This time use No. 400 wet-or-dry and continue to use a sanding block. After this is done you may find a few places where it is necessary to do a little more filling with the glazing compound. After all the sanding is done, you are ready for the final coat of paint. Remember that the paint will not cover up mistakes or fill any holes. The surface must be as smooth before the final coat as you would like to have it after the final coat.

Finish with two coats of enamel and wet-sand without a block with No. 400 paper between coats. The drying time before sanding the enamel will vary greatly with the temperature and thickness of the enamel but will generally be not less than 24 hours and may be over 48 hours. Do not rush the final sanding—and be careful of all corners—it is easy to go through the enamel and impossible to do a perfect job of touching up as the spot will almost always show.

The best finish will be secured by polishing with rubbing compound (available at any auto paint store), but this should not be attempted until the paint has set a month, as the solvent in the compound sometimes softens new paint. This gives you time to ponder over the advantages of joining the wettable surface crowd, which advocates another sanding instead of polishing.

In case you have bought a new automobile and your wife is tired of the color scheme of your old boat and thinks you should paint the boat to match the color of the new car, don't just go down to the dealer and pick up some of the automobile paint to do it. If your new car is one of the makes which is painted with enamel, this is fine; but if it is one of the makes which is painted with lacquer, you may get into a lot of trouble trying to put lacquer on top of enamel.

If the enamel is fairly new, chances are pretty good that the lacquer will simply lift the enamel in large areas of bubbles. If the enamel is old, the lacquer will probably start peeling off after a month or two. Du Pont and, I presume, many other paint companies make enamel to match all of the lacquer colors used by the automobile companies, and it is better to use the enamel and be safe instead of sorry.

There are, probably, still a few things that I haven't done wrong at one time or another in doing my own spray painting on a boat, but I don't think there are too many. I am convinced that the best thing to do is to take the boat to an automobile paint shop and let them do the job. Listed below are some of the better mouse-traps to avoid if you insist on doing your own painting.

One of the most important things is to thin the enamel properly, using a fast-drying thinner if you are spraying in cool or cold weather. Don't try to make any improvement on the percentage of thinner recommended by the paint manufacturer. If it doesn't flow through the gun properly, don't just add more thinner hoping that will make it work. The chances are that either the vent hole in the suction cup is closed up or that one of the small internal passages is plugged up if the gun does not spray properly with the recommended amount of thinner. Even when the paint comes from a brand-new can and has been thoroughly stirred, it should be strained through a regular paint strainer or a discarded nylon stocking, because there are bound to be small pieces of undissolved pigment which will stop up the gun.

If you try to spray with too much thinner, the enamel will go on beautifully but it won't cover very well and, in an effort to make it cover, you will get nice big sags.

The other extreme of not using enough thinner will produce even more disastrous results. When you have used too much thinner, at least the paint dries rapidly and you can sand out the sags and start over again; however, if you use too little thinner with the theory that you will use higher pressure and get more paint on faster and cover better, you will accomplish all of that, except the stuff won't dry before next summer sometime.

Even with the proper mixture, the amateur spray painting only occasionally has difficulty in deciding how close to hold the gun to the surface being sprayed. If the gun is held too close, particularly when the surface has quite a slope, the material will be very wet when it goes on with a tendency towards sagging. If the gun is held too far away, sags will be avoided but the final paint job will have a lot of orange peel in it and will require a lot of sanding to look good. (The best way to do this job is still to take it to an automobile paint shop.)

One thing on which everyone agrees is that no polishing should be done on new enamel in less than a month and preferably six weeks. Some people say that the enamel can be sanded sooner than that and others say no. If you get a perfect paint job—which you are more likely to get by letting an automobile body shop do the job with automobile refinish enamel—you may decide not to sand the final job at all. It is possible, but not easy, to get a paint job practically free of orange peel, and yet without sags and runs, which really needs no final sanding. It won't be quite as good as the finish on the finest grand pianos, but can be very acceptable.

If you have decided to use metallic pigmented enamel, it is a good idea to decide at the same time to let a professional spray it. Another thing that may convince you to let an automobile paint shop do your next job is having the female member of the family find overspray on some highly treasured stuff stored in the garage which looked like junk to you and therefore you didn't cover it.

9

Protests and Protest Committees

EVERY NOW AND THEN AFTER A REGATTA, THE REGATTA COMMITTEE WILL congratulate itself because it has had a regatta without protests. If there have been no fouls which should have been protested, this is a fine record; but, if there have been fouls which should have been protested and if people go home griping about fouls which were committed and not protested, it is certainly nothing to brag about.

There is no sport in which sportsmanship is on as high a level as it is in sailboat racing; but, in my opinion, it is actually poor sportsmanship to not protest a foul which should be protested, particularly if the person against whom the foul was committed goes around griping that so-and-so fouled him but he didn't protest because it didn't affect his position.

There are some inadvertent and unavoidable fouls which are not a result of taking a chance with the rules in the hope of gaining an advantage. These, I think, should not be protested; they also should not be griped about.

If, however, you think that you have been fouled by another boat and the foul is not one of the excusable types just mentioned, the only sportsman-like thing to do is to protest and get the thing settled.

Fouls generally result from stretching luck too far in order to gain some advantage or in order to not sacrifice a position. A person doing this takes a calculated risk; and if he doesn't make it, it is not fair to others who have been more cautious not to protest.

Fouls sometimes result from people just not knowing the rules —or knowing them wrong. A protest is the only way to convince this type of offender that he should stop doing what he has been doing.

It also happens rather frequently that the person who thinks he was fouled doesn't know the rules himself, and no foul was actually committed. In this case, if the person who thinks he was fouled doesn't protest, but goes around griping that he was fouled, he is not giving the alleged offender his right to trial by jury (the protest committee in this case); he is, in effect, trying his alleged offender in the headlines like some of our senatorial committees used to do.

It isn't necessary to mention that it is extremely poor sportsmanship to go around looking for opportunities to tag someone out, and I feel as though even if it is not required in the rules, it is good sportsmanship to hail another skipper when you have the right of way and it looks like you might get tangled up with him. I know I have been saved from trouble on several occasions and have been very grateful to a starboard tacker who showed up in a spot where I was sure no starboard tacker could be and who hailed me before I plowed into him on a port tack.

Small regattas should, and important regattas must, have a protest committee that knows what it is doing. The protest committee, like the skippers, should not go out of their way to cook up means of disqualifying people, but, on the other hand, they should not shirk their responsibility when a protest is filed and they should act promptly and firmly on any protest.

The advent of the alternate penalty systems has made people less reluctant to protest but there are still some who don't protest or call for the execution of a 720 and then gripe about the alleged foul later. Incidentally, don't forget that if there is any contact no matter how minor between hull, equipment, or crew of two boats, one of them must protest or accept an alternate penalty. If the incident is very minor, the protest committee does not have to disqualify anyone if either boat files a protest. If neither boat complies completely with all the requirements of the rule on protests, both boats must be disqualified. The protest committee has no option in this case.

10

Helpful Hints to Regatta Committees

SINCE THE PREVAILING WEATHER AT REGATTAS IS ALWAYS LOUSY, THE science of winning friends and influencing people among regatta contestants consists of making them want to come back again in spite of the things that couldn't be helped because of the excellence of things about which something could be done.

In an effort to compile a Dale Carnegie course for regatta committees, I have catalogued all of the important regattas which I have sailed in or watched, listing their exceptionally good and exceptionally bad features, and I came to the conclusion that with very few exceptions they could have been improved to some degree by giving a little more consideration to the fact which should be obvious but seems to frequently get lost in the shuffle—namely, that the visiting skippers like to have a good time, but primarily came to the regatta to race!

This lack of consideration usually arises from the fact that, while a few of the local skippers have attended equally important regattas, the majority of the members with whom they have to work have not, and their advice is generally ignored to varying degrees. Because these skippers who have been around still have to continue working and living with the other people involved, they are generally browbeaten into submission. However, since anything that appears in print automatically acquires a ring of authenticity, maybe in the future the suggestions contained here will help racing skippers who are working on regattas and are having a little trouble convincing other members of their clubs that things should be different on regatta day.

RACE COURSES

Most of the trouble with courses arises due to the fact that courses and starting lines which provide the best racing conditions frequently cause inconvenience for the racing committee and the spectators. In purely local races, since race committees are extremely hard to come by, life is generally made as easy for them as possible because their job is a thankless one at best. Also, the spectators on the club porch or float are generally families of skippers and crews or other club members, who, as cash customers, consider themselves entitled to a grandstand seat where they can see the start and finish of the race.

These are perfectly valid considerations when laying out the starting lines and courses for local races, but they must be tossed in the ash can if you want to make friends and influence people among skippers who have come hundreds or thousands of miles in order to sail a series of races.

Permanently located markers almost invariably cause trouble. In the first place, some concessions have probably been made to the convenience of the spectators and the race committee in locating them. In the second place, the fact that the wind always blows from a certain direction insures only that the marks will be in the wrong place when you put on a regatta, because the wind always blows from a direction in which it has never blown before as soon as the regatta starts. Unless it is absolutely impossible because of depth of water, light buoys which can be shifted should be used. A very satisfactory buoy can be made from an automobile inner tube with a bushel basket inverted on top of the inner tube and painted with fluorescent paint and with a flag made of daylight fluorescent fabric about 3 feet above the bushel basket.

A fluttering flag is much easier to find than a cone on top of a pole, and the bushel basket, being considerably larger than any cone that can be put on top of a pole, also makes the mark stand out very well. The buoy should be weighted slightly to hold the pole perpendicular, and the mooring line should be weighted also so that it will run as nearly as possible vertically downward from the buoy.

In any regatta, everyone agrees that all starts must be made to windward, but frequently not as much is done about it as might be. When a skipper has come a long way to sail in a regatta, he will not mind going downwind from the clubhouse a mile or so in order to get a full windward leg rather than to settle for a short beat to the first mark from a starting line more conveniently located. This generally involves beating the spectators out of a chance to see the start and involves a deviation from standard local practice, but it is a very important thing to do even in a relatively unimportant regatta if you want to convince the skippers that the contestants are more important than the spectators. On small lakes, it is frequently difficult to get any cooperation out of the wind and some rather weird courses may be necessary, but nobody objects to these providing maximum use is made of the available water in providing a beat after the start.

When the starting line is likely to be a long way from the anchorage, it is a good idea to announce this fact far enough ahead of time so that boats have no excuse for not being there on time, and then the race should be started promptly at the advertised time. One of the regattas around this part of the country which used to be very popular has just about lost all of its customers because they never seem to be able to do anything on time. The last time I was there was several years ago, the wind was blowing between 30 and 35 miles an hour, and the starting line was about a mile from the anchorage. I got out to the starting line along with several other boats about 15 minutes before the scheduled start and had an hour and 20 minutes' practice at reaching and bailing before the race started.

There are, however, times when it is even more important to postpone a race than it is to have it on time. This is in case the wind has shifted so that what was intended to be a beat at the start has suddenly become a reach or a run or a one-tack beat to the first mark. As soon as this happens, a postponement gun should be fired and, in these cases, it should be made clear that the postponement will not be for any fixed time interval and that the 10-minute gun will be fired as soon as the race committee has made another guess on where the wind is going to be and establishes a new course and a new starting line.

I have seen cases where one minute you would lay the mark on one tack and the next minute lay it on the opposite tack. In a case like this, if there is enough breeze so the race won't be a drifting match, about all that can be done is hit the average wind direction as well as possible and go ahead and hope; however, there is nothing more destructive to a visiting skipper's morale than having to start out on a leeward-leeward course or one in which no tacking is necessary on the alleged windward leg. He wants to get things started on time, but he would much rather sit around for awhile waiting for the course to be shifted than to start out on a course where there will be no windward leg or no tacking.

When sailing a triangular course, a reverse course signal is extremely handy, providing its use has been explained at the skippers' meeting. It is not nearly as confusing as it seems like it might be, and on several occasions I have seen it used to make a good race out of what would have otherwise degenerated into a follow-the-leader reaching contest.

The desired length of the course varies directly with the importance of the regatta, with the maximum length courses being desirable at the more important regattas where a large number of skippers have come a long way in order to sail. The courses should always be at least two laps in order to minimize the effect of tricky local conditions which may have trapped some of the skippers in the first lap.

STARTING LINES

Good starting lines are just as important as good courses, and they seem to be much harder to get. If a fixed starting line is normally used, such as one between a buoy and the end of the dock or a flagpole, any idea of using this in a regatta should be promptly forgotten. The chances are that at best some compromise is involved in either the direction or the location of the starting line, and, in any case, when the regatta comes, the wind is sure not to cooperate, so starts should always be planned to take place between a committee boat and a buoy and it is highly desirable to have another boat near the end of the line opposite to the committee boat to help in getting the numbers of early starters.

The larger the committee boat, the poorer the chances are of having a good starting line, because the larger the boat is, the harder it is to move when you want to move it or to keep from moving when you want it to stay put. Since it is almost inevitable that the line will have to be changed several times (especially if the committee boat tries to establish the line well ahead of time), an attempt should be made to browbeat the race committee into accepting the smallest possible committee boat with the biggest possible assortment of anchors and lines so that it can be moved easily and quickly in order to give a good line.

The only way I know of to tell whether or not a starting line is perfect is to have sailed around in the vicinity of the starting line long enough to know what the compass course is on the average starboard tack close-hauled, and then to take a compass bearing on the starting line. It is extremely difficult to establish a good starting line by merely watching a flag on the committee boat and sighting on the buoy on the other end of the line, and I don't know why so many race committees consider it a reflection on their ability to ask a contestant whether or not the line is all right.

When the wind is shifty (and when isn't it?), it is admittedly difficult to establish a starting line which will stay perfect up to the time of the actual start. The starting line can be moved, however, at any time up to the 5-minute gun and frequently a little pulling in or letting out on the anchor line on the committee boat will accomplish wonders in keeping the sailors happy; and if the line really goes sour, no skipper is going to complain about a postponement signal any time prior to the start in order to improve the line. It is amazing the way some race committees turn a deaf ear to skippers screaming at them when the only similarity between what they have set out for a starting line and the correct one is that you have to stay behind both of them until the starting signal. The race committee doesn't lose any prestige by admitting that its line is sour—it loses prestige only by forcing the skippers to believe that it doesn't know what a starting line should be by its actions, or lack of them.

When it is necessary to go a long way for a good windward start, no one will complain if the course has otherwise been good. In any regatta of national or international importance the course should be a standard Olympic course—triangle, windward, leeward, windward. Any inconvenience of the skippers having to go a long way to the course can be greatly lessened by providing power boats to tow them if the wind is light.

A perfect starting line could probably be defined as one on which an experienced skipper without a compass would be unable to make up his mind as to which end of the line would be best. This can be accomplished very simply by having the line square to the wind. If the angle between the starting line and the starboard tack is more than 45 degrees there will be a large gangup at the windward end of the line. Since, in most cases, the wind is not steady enough to permit having an absolutely perfect starting line, it is better to err on the side of giving the port end more than it should have, but only by a few degrees.

Since marks will be left to port if at all possible, the committee boat will be (or at least should be—some race committees are a little casual on this) on the windward end of the line and a long anchor line will not interfere with the boats. If the wind is showing a consistent shift in one direction, an estimated amount of shift can be allowed for prior to the 5-minute gun so that the line will be practically perfect at the starting gun.

The nervous tension is always high prior to the start of a race in an important regatta, and the racing skippers will remember the starting line long after they have forgotten everything else about the event.

There is no fixed rule as to the length of starting lines; however, a minimum is a little more than the total length of all the boats in the race. Lines much longer than this should be avoided simply because of the fact that the advantage occurring at one end or the other tends to be accentuated by a longer starting line.

It is important that the committee boat should be on the proper end of the finish line and the finish line should be very carefully established so that it is absolutely at right angles to the course from the last mark, or at right angles to the wind direction if the finish is to windward. The line should be long enough to accommodate a fairly large number of boats trying to cross it at the same time, generally one-half, or less, the length of the starting line. There is also no big mystery as to the proper end of the line for the committee boat on either the start or the finish. The rule is very simply that all buoys are left on the same side. If marks are to be left to port, the buoy should be left to port on the start and also the finish line.

STARTING PROCEDURE

Guns have a habit of going off when they shouldn't and not going off when they should, but everybody is accustomed to this and as long as the visual signals are correct only a minor amount of confusion will result from misbehaving guns. However, when the 5-minute signal is not exactly 5 minutes after the 10-minute signal, the possibilities of confusion are terrific. The rules require that each succeeding signal be made at the correct interval from the preceding signal, and a postponement is recommended when an interval is incorrect. When the 5-minute signal has been made at an incorrect time interval after the 10-minute signal, the race committee generally knows about it and, if they don't, they will soon be informed of their error by frantic screams from the contestants. Unfortunately, many race committees exercise their prerogative of ignoring the contestants and letting them guess what's going to happen next.

Since getting a properly timed start is one of the measures of skill in sailboat racing, the only fair thing to do is to make a postponement signal and start over again. Some people may have missed the 10-minute signal and have been counting on timing their start from the 5-minute signal, so that, even if the race committee gets honest and admits its 5-minute signal was haywire, they still may have eliminated the possibility of a number of boats getting a well-timed start through no fault of the contestant.

11

Psychology in Sailboat Racing

PSYCHOLOGY IS THE SCIENCE OF THE MIND, AND IT STUDIES THE BEHAVIOR of people. A discussion of psychology in sailboat racing involves a consideration of what effect the skipper's mental attitude may have on his racing performance. In my opinion, the effect is, in many cases, an extremely important one; and is a very appropriate subject to look at in the final chapter of *Scientific Sailboat Racing.*

You have all seen skippers who sail a perfect race now and then and a perfect series of races less often, but who never seem to end up on top at the end of the season. If these skippers could sail every race as well as they do some races they would be unbeatable. There is also another group of skippers who can make their boats go just as fast as anyone's boat when they are merely playing around or sailing in some race which has no importance, but who never manage to make the grade in tough competition.

Luck, of course, enters into these performances to some extent, but in the long run the breaks will be about even and it must be something else that causes this kind of result. This something else is the state of mind or mental attitude of the skipper.

The mental attitude of the skipper who wins consistently must always be one of complete confidence in the ability of his boat and his sails to win the race if he only handles them right; courage tempered with just the right amount of conservatism (an excess of either of these will get him into trouble); and a calm and cool appraisal of the constantly changing situations arising during a race. (I didn't really try to pick words all of which began with "c," but it turns out that way, and should make the lesson easier to remember.)

Confidence consists of constantly remembering that you have proven on numerous occasions that you can go just as fast as the other boats, on many occasions that you can go faster, and being convinced that you are going to win the race.

Courage consists of taking calculated risks when the odds look good enough, after applying just enough conservatism to be sure that you are being courageous and not just plain reckless, when it comes to picking a good spot on the starting line even though it is crowded; tacking for a safe leeward position instead of going behind another boat; cutting inside of a boat on a mark when it has rounded it sloppily, etc.

Coolness consists of keeping off the panic button when things don't go exactly the way you planned them, and remembering constantly that the race is not over until you cross the finish line and a regatta series is neither won nor lost until the last race is finished.

The last stage at which you will arrive before winning regattas consistently, and the first one at which you will arrive when you start losing your touch after winning some regattas, will be this nautical equivalent of being always a bridesmaid but never a bride.

The secret of success in winning tune-up races and losing regattas is to start doing stupid things under pressure. The best way to accomplish this is to not do enough racing. Reading or writing articles on how to win races or just pleasure sailing won't take the place of being in races. It has often been said that the best way to win a race is to get out in front at the start and steadily improve your position. Quite a few regattas are won this way because there is a definite advantage in being out in front; however, the racing competition in big regattas has gotten so stiff that even the skippers who are likely to win the regattas get bottled up occasionally on starts or take tacks which turn out to be sour and have to work their way up through the fleet; and the ones who win the most regattas are the ones who can't be counted on to stay bottled up when their situation looks hopeless.

One of the temptations hardest to resist is to immediately tack out and get clear after a mediocre start. Under these conditions, the wind in which you are sailing is badly scrambled up by boats ahead of you and the water is the same way. It is far better to just sit there and make the best of it for awhile until things settle down. If you can only resist that temptation long enough, it is amazing how many other people succumb to it and how much better off you are by just staying put (barring wind shifts, of course).

The next hardest temptation to resist is to keep going on a tack which has become sour because immediate tacking will put you behind some other boats. There is a terrific temptation to go just a little bit farther so as to be clear before tacking. The trouble is that you generally have to go farther than you anticipate before you get clear, and all of the time that you are persisting on this tack, you are going in the wrong direction in relation to the people ahead of you that you hope to eventually overhaul.

The next thing that happens after succumbing to the above two temptations is to push the panic button. When you have done this, you start trimming your sails too tightly because everyone else seems to be pointing higher than you are; you start trying to go to windward by just aiming there; you start doing things quickly and jerkily instead of slowly and smoothly, and every tack you get on seems to be the wrong one so you come about again.

That it takes Confidence, Courage, and Coolness has all been proven to be true, but unfortunately the whole thing is a bit easier said than done. A knowledge of technique and tactics learned by experience plus constant effort to improve while sailing in as many races as possible in as tough competition as you can find is the solution to the problem.